the Smithsonian FIRST LADIES *collection*

LISA KATHLEEN GRADDY
and AMY PASTAN

the Smithsonian
FIRST
LADIES
collection

SMITHSONIAN BOOKS   WASHINGTON, DC

CONTENTS

OPPOSITE: Caroline Harrison's evening gown.
PREVIOUS SPREAD: Inaugural gowns worn by Laura Bush in 2001 (left) and Rosalynn Carter in 1977 (right).

First ladies are unofficial but important members of presidential administrations. For more than two hundred years we have judged their clothes, their parties, their projects, and their roles and influence in the White House. While some duties, such as hostess of the Executive Mansion, are performed by all first ladies, the job does not come with a specific list of responsibilities. Over different times and circumstances, every first lady has fashioned her own way of handling the White House and families, parties, politics, and public scrutiny. Each has crafted significant roles for herself that she believed would allow her to suit her own interests, the needs of the presidential administration, and the public's changing expectations of women in general and first ladies in particular.

The Smithsonian's First Ladies Collection weaves its famous gowns into a look at how these very different women have approached their undefined yet challenging position. This presentation is just the most recent incarnation of the beloved

ABOVE: Cassie Mason Myers Julian-James (left) and Rose Gouverneur Hoes (right), the founders of the First Ladies Collection, dress a mannequin in a gown worn by Louisa Catherine Adams, 1916.

exhibition that has been one of the Smithsonian's most popular attractions for more than a hundred years. Much like the women it presents, the exhibition has been repeatedly reimagined. Curators have experimented with new ways of expanding and interpreting the beloved collection to explore the mix of celebrity and achievement, fashion, and power that makes the history of the first ladies endlessly fascinating to visitors. The exhibition also addresses a question that has long puzzled Smithsonian staff: Why is there such interest in what the first ladies wear?

The idea for the collection began as a rainy day project more than a century ago. When dreary weather prevented Cassie Mason Myers Julian-James, a Washington society figure and museum enthusiast, from taking her ailing mother on their regular afternoon drive, they instead whiled away the afternoon by talking about a trunk filled with clothes and beautiful keepsakes that Mrs. James's grandmother had stored away in a New England attic. Mother and daughter decided they would each add a complete ensemble of their own to the trunk and create a small collection of women's fashion that spanned a century.[1]

Mrs. James, a frequent donor to the Smithsonian, shared the story of her grandmother's trunk with museum staff, and they urged her to exhibit her collection there. She readily agreed and soon proposed expanding the small display into a larger exhibition of historic American clothing. The well-connected leader of Washington society turned volunteer curator began to solicit support—and clothes—from her wide network of friends. Rose Gouverneur Hoes, the great-granddaughter of President James Monroe, contributed Monroe family relics—and an idea. Together Hoes and James developed a plan for a gallery of women's clothing featuring the "costumes of the ladies of the White House."[2] Some of the families they contacted were reluctant to participate in the project. An Adams descendant remarked that "his ancestors were not in the habit of keeping their old clothes."[3] Mary Lincoln's family "displayed no especial interest,"[4] and recent First Lady Edith Roosevelt refused to send a gown since "she could not understand why the public was clamoring for her dress."[5] Still, by

unique for this country in its largeness of scope and in part at least for its method of presentation."

— Annual Report of the National Museum, 1914

the time the exhibition, titled Collection of Period Costumes, made its public debut on February 1, 1914, Hoes and James had received gowns contributed by the friends and families of fifteen former first ladies.

The most important "yes" came from Helen Taft, who was then first lady. In 1912 she contributed the gown she had worn to her husband's inaugural ball three years earlier. Her enthusiastic support of the exhibition, coupled with its immediate popularity, prompted others to loan or donate missing gowns. This encouraged James to believe the exhibition would continue to grow, "giving the public a most valuable collection of historic costumes of the great women of our country of whom we are so justly proud."[6] Indeed, Mrs. Taft's donation established a precedent for future first ladies. Since that time, each first lady who attended an inaugural ball for her husband has donated the gown she wore to the event.

The cases featuring the first ladies' gowns quickly became one of the museum's most popular attractions. Women crowded the new exhibition, fascinated by the beautiful clothes and the inclusion of the first ladies as role models and historical figures. The collection expanded as more donations of memorabilia arrived and as the gown of each outgoing first lady was added to the display. In 1931 the exhibition moved to a more spacious gallery on the other side of the hall, where "the collections illustrating Power, assembled by the division of mechanical technology, are proving an attraction for the male visitors, offsetting the 'feminine' display on the right."[7] The new presentation may have been beautiful and genteel, but woman power was competing with mechanical power in its ability to attract visitors.

Margaret Brown (later Klapthor) became the curator of the First Ladies Collection in 1943, when male members of the Smithsonian staff "didn't

ABOVE: First ladies' gowns displayed in the Collection of Period Costumes exhibition, about 1930. In keeping with standard museum practice at the time, the labels included brief identifications but no biographical information about the women or detailed descriptions of the dresses. OVERLEAF: The Blue Room period setting in Margaret Klapthor's *First Ladies Hall*, about 1970.

want to mess around with those dresses."[8] She made the most of the opportunity and drew on the popularity of period rooms to create a stunning new gallery for the first ladies. More lifelike mannequins were grouped in sets modeled after historic rooms in the White House, where architectural elements salvaged from President Harry Truman's recent renovation of the Executive Mansion heightened the feeling of authenticity. Klapthor's decorative arts approach expanded the collection to include larger displays of jewelry, accessories, and White House china and furnishings. While the spectacular exhibition depicted the changing style of the White House and the evolving social role of the first lady, the gowns remained the main attraction. The public's keen desire to see Mamie Eisenhower's inaugural dress prompted a new tradition. Instead of waiting until the Eisenhowers left the White House, as had been done up to that time, Klapthor displayed the current first lady's famous pink ball gown in the final period room. She also invited Mrs. Eisenhower to attend the formal opening of the renovated exhibition hall in 1955.

Clothing, especially when displayed on mannequins, can help make even the most distant historical figure feel closer to the viewer. It conveys an impression of a person's physical presence, and it can illustrate the personal style of a first lady or the official style of a presidential administration. Unfortunately, long years on exhibition damaged many of the beloved gowns. When a major construction project in the museum led to the removal of the period rooms, Smithsonian curators were encouraged to take the presentation of the collection in a different direction, one that centered on the first ladies' actions and accomplishments while in office. In 1992 curator Edith Mayo developed a bold new exhibition based on political and social history. *First Ladies: Political Role and Public*

Image shifted the focus to the women's evolving roles and contributions to American politics and culture. The first ladies' work—and not their clothes— took center stage. Campaign buttons and popular souvenirs joined the traditional cases of jewelry and china in an examination of their roles as social advocates, hostesses, political campaigners, and presidential partners. Conservators treated the dresses and created new mannequins to support the fragile fabrics, which enabled fourteen dresses to go back on display in a separate gallery designed to minimize damage from light, dust, and climate. Some visitors missed the unbroken parade of gowns, but most welcomed the updated look at the influence and power of the first ladies. Since then, other versions of the exhibition have explored the history of the collection and the "debut" of the new first lady at the inaugural ball. The most recent installation pairs an exploration of the approach different first ladies take to their role with an examination of the continuing public interest in what they wear.

Judging by the crowds in the galleries, the First Ladies Collection is as popular as ever. For millions of tourists every year, a trip to the Smithsonian is not complete without a visit to see the first ladies' gowns. In many ways the legendary collection has become an American icon and a treasured memory for generations of museum goers.

In this book we share some of the objects that the Smithsonian has used over the past century to document the lives and achievements of America's first ladies. Many people marvel at the exhibition's enduring popularity, but its founders would not have been surprised at the lasting success of the Smithsonian's first exhibition created specifically by, for, and about women. What began as a rainy day entertainment has evolved into a source of pride and inspiration that both highlights the contributions of these often overlooked leaders and asks visitors, What would you do with the job if it were yours?

LISA KATHLEEN GRADDY —Curator, Division of Political History, Smithsonian National Museum of American History

OPPOSITE: In the 2011 exhibition *The First Ladies*, "highboy" cases examine the approach of different first ladies to their role in the White House.

ABOVE: The introductory case in the current installation addresses an enduring question: Why is the public interested in what the first lady wears?

TOP ROW, LEFT: Emily Donelson, niece of Andrew Jackson; CENTER: Martha Jefferson Randolph, daughter of Thomas Jefferson; RIGHT: Sarah Yorke Jackson, daughter-in-law of Andrew Jackson

BOTTOM ROW, LEFT: Martha Johnson Patterson, daughter of Andrew Johnson; CENTER: Angelica Singleton Van Buren, daughter-in-law of Martin Van Buren; RIGHT: Betty Taylor Bliss, daughter of Zachary Taylor

Since the founding of the United States, every president has had an official hostess. Without one, propriety into the twentieth century forbade the president from including women—the wives of congressmen and diplomats, for instance—at his parties and receptions. Since these social occasions provide opportunities for the president to build international relationships, win political friends, or further his legislative agenda, a hostess has been a vital member of his administration. If the president was a bachelor or a widower, or if his wife was unable or uninterested in filling the role of hostess, he chose another female family member or friend to serve that purpose. Daughters, daughters-in-law, nieces, and sisters have acted as the hostess of the White House. Among these women are Betty Bliss, the daughter of Zachary Taylor; Angelica Van Buren, the daughter-in-law of Martin Van Buren; Emily Donelson, the niece of Andrew Jackson; Mary McElroy, the sister of Chester Arthur; and even Dolley Madison, who, as a friend of the president and wife of the secretary of state, served as a hostess for Thomas Jefferson. While all of these women ably assisted as hostesses, only Harriet Lane, the niece of James Buchanan, enjoyed the long-term political partnership that characterizes the role of first lady.

When the Smithsonian set about creating the display that eventually became the First Ladies Collection, these women were included as a way to represent each presidential administration. In 1931 Rose Gouverneur Hoes, a founder of the collection, justified the inclusions as a practical necessity: "It is not an exhibition of the dresses of the wives of the Presidents, but the gowns of the mistresses of the White House. If it were the former there would be many vacancies in this long line of historical costumes."[1] As the exhibition moved away from a chronological display of dresses and toward an exploration of the variety of roles played by first ladies, less attention was focused on some of these "mistresses of the White House," and the collections related to them have not grown. Their inclusion in the original 1914 exhibition, however, shaped the Smithsonian's historic "definition" of a first lady as the woman who acted as the official White House hostess during a presidential administration.

What will happen when one day the president is a woman? She will have to reconsider the duties of the "first lady" and decide whether she expects her husband, a family member, or others to assume this role in her administration. The Smithsonian will follow her lead in determining who is added to the exhibition, and the definition of "first lady" will undoubtedly change.

ABOVE: When they could not locate a gown for either Anna Harrison or her daughter to represent the administration of William Henry Harrison, Hoes and James added a dress worn by Jane Findlay, a family friend who assisted with the first lady's duties.

The textile conservation lab at the National Museum of American History is populated with seemingly ghostly forms. They are mannequins created for exhibiting the costumes from the museum's collection, including the dresses and inaugural gowns of the first ladies. Among the most popular items at the museum, the gowns require very special care. Senior Costume Conservator Sunae Park Evans is at once a scientist and an artist, pairing specialized scientific knowledge of conservation analysis with the ability to create the historically accurate forms that support the dresses worn by America's first ladies. She is acquainted with these women in an intimate way: she knows their measurements, favorite colors, fashion taste, and personal style.

Dr. Evans compares this field of conservation to that of health care. Not long ago doctors treated patients only when they became ill, and conservators used to repair objects only when they became damaged. Now, just as doctors try to practice preventive medical care so their patients live healthier and longer lives, so conservators attempt to protect fragile historic costumes before they show any signs of degradation. This involves gently cleaning the items with a vacuum cleaner set at low speed when necessary, storing them with proper supports in a controlled environment, and keeping them from light exposure that causes fading. Even though the items on display are kept at a low light level, they are still vulnerable because textiles are one of the materials most sensitive to light damage. In another preventive conservation measure, the museum plans to rotate the dresses on exhibit every three to six months to protect them for future generations.

Mannequins made of Ethafoam, a lightweight, inert material that is easy to handle and adjust to size, help the dresses to be supported properly and hold their shape while on display. Dr. Evans builds and mounts a mannequin for each costume. (The mounts are left headless to focus attention on the garment.) She sometimes uses a muslin pattern of the original dress to minimize handling of the fragile historic object. This process also ensures

the costume appears accurate by furnishing the correct body shape and stance for the time period. In this way the mounts created for the first ladies' dresses provide a sense of how the costumes would have been worn. Lucy Hayes's Victorian gown—with high neck, long sleeves, and bustle—was certainly more constricting than Michelle Obama's flowing, bare-armed creation by Jason Wu.

Due to their fragile fabric condition, the most challenging dresses to conserve are generally the oldest ones, such as the eighteenth-century dresses of Martha Washington and Dolley Madison, but newer clothes present unique problems as well. The weighted silk used in nineteenth-century gowns becomes weak and fragile over time, as seen in Caroline Harrison's brocaded inaugural dress of 1889. Garments made of the silk soon shred and

RIGHT: Senior Costume Conservator Sunae Park Evans fits a muslin underdress and stay on an Ethafoam form prior to clothing the mannequin in a dress worn by Martha Washington.

sometimes become powdery. Mamie Eisenhower's pink rhinestone-studded dress of the 1950s has already lost some of its sparkle. The thread used to sew on the heavy rhinestones degraded, and eventually the stones came loose. Dr. Evans believes it is better to handle the objects as little as possible. Repairs of old fragile fabric could actually lead to more damage, as a needle would introduce holes into the already delicate fabric and could further weaken areas.

What is Dr. Evans's favorite dress in the First Ladies Collection? She finds it hard to settle on just one. Nancy Reagan's single-shoulder gown by James Galanos is beautifully constructed, and Martha Washington's dress crafted of hand-painted silk is a wonderful example of eighteenth-century textile art. Dr. Evans admires the simple elegance of Eleanor Roosevelt's pale green ball gown, but she is most impressed by the high taste and fashionably modern style of the nation's youngest first lady, Frances Cleveland. She can see how the rich colors and careful tailoring of Mrs. Cleveland's clothes created a sensation when she debuted them in the late nineteenth century.

Several of the first ladies who donated their inaugural gowns to the Smithsonian Institution have admitted that they had a difficult time parting with the dress that represented one of the most important moments in their lives. Clothing holds memories, and because it is so personal, it may reveal aspects of a person that otherwise go undocumented. That is why Dr. Evans and other conservators work hard to get the details right. History is not an abstraction of the past. It's real.

MICHELLE ROBINSON OBAMA

Michelle Obama impressed the public during her husband's 2008 presidential campaign and has brought charm and elegance to the White House. The nation's first African American first lady maintains an active calendar, leading fitness classes at schools, harvesting vegetables in the White House organic garden, and being "first mom" to her daughters Sasha and Malia. She is committed to the future of the nation's children, founding Let's Move! to encourage healthy eating and to challenge the problem of childhood obesity in this country. In addition, she cofounded, with Dr. Jill Biden, the vice president's wife, the Joining Forces program to support military families.

Michelle was born in 1964 on the South Side of Chicago. Her dad worked as a pump operator, and her mom stayed home to raise Michelle and her brother. Michelle attended public school, studied at Princeton University, and graduated from Harvard Law School in 1988. She met Barack Obama while working at a law firm, and they were married in 1992. Michelle applied her knowledge of law to serve diverse communities. She eventually became vice president of community and external affairs for the University of Chicago Medical Center until she left her position to assume the role of first lady.

During her husband's second term in the White House, Michelle has continued to speak out on behalf of women's issues, encourage national service, and promote a healthy lifestyle. She wrote *American Grown: The Story of the White House Kitchen Garden and Gardens Across America* and also initiated an annual Kids State Dinner for school-age winners of a challenge to create a healthy recipe.

ABOVE LEFT: Queen Elizabeth II welcomes the Obamas to Buckingham Palace on April 1, 2009. ABOVE RIGHT: Michelle Obama congratulates a graduating high school senior in Nashville on May 18, 2013.
RIGHT: The first lady participates in a Let's Move! event with National Football League players in New Orleans on September 8, 2010.
OPPOSITE: Michelle Obama wore this silk chiffon gown with organza flowers to the 2009 inaugural balls. Designer Jason Wu intended it to symbolize hope.

TOP LEFT: Loree Rodkin designed Michelle Obama's jewelry for the inaugural balls. These triple rose-cut diamond earrings, with a center cluster of diamond briolettes, are set in white gold; total carat weight of 61.9. TOP RIGHT: Mrs. Obama presents her gown to the First Ladies Collection in March 2010.

BOTTOM LEFT: "Michelle" signet ring of white gold and black rhodium with rose-cut diamonds around a rose-cut diamond center stone; total carat weight of 13. BOTTOM RIGHT: White satin shoes by Jimmy Choo.

OPPOSITE: Mrs. Obama's silk chiffon dress was the first inaugural ball gown with a train in sixty-four years.

LAURA WELCH BUSH

A former teacher and librarian, Laura Bush used her eight years as first lady to promote education and reading. She supported her husband's education reform program—No Child Left Behind—and founded her own initiative—Ready to Read, Ready to Learn—to aid teachers and children. She hosted the first annual National Book Festival in Washington, which was inspired by the Texas Book Festival she began when she was first lady of that state.

Laura promoted women's health and education worldwide, meeting leaders for a Global Literacy Conference in 2006 and traveling to Afghanistan to visit schools there. Quiet and poised, she was the first first lady to deliver the president's weekly radio address. She used the opportunity to speak out against the Taliban rule in Afghanistan and its oppression of women and children. She was also outspoken on human rights violations in Myanmar. Although her husband's first term was marked by the terrorist attacks on September 11, 2001, she remained a comforting presence during the crisis.

Born in 1946 in Midland, Texas, Laura Welch graduated from Southern Methodist University with a degree in education and earned a master's degree in library science at the University of Texas at Austin. She wed George W. Bush in 1977, and they had twin daughters in 1981. Laura married into a politically active family, with her in-laws Barbara and George H. W. Bush having served as first lady and president a decade earlier.

After leaving the White House, Laura wrote a memoir and worked with her husband on opening the George W. Bush Presidential Center in 2013. They currently live near Dallas, Texas.

ABOVE: Laura Bush arrives at the Aschiani School in Kabul, Afghanistan, on March 30, 2005.
LEFT: For the Bush White House china, Mrs. Bush chose a Lenox service with a green border because it complemented a variety of colored table linens and flower arrangements.
BOTTOM CENTER: Button from the 2000 presidential campaign.
OPPOSITE: For the 2001 inaugural balls, Mrs. Bush wore this ruby-red gown of crystal-embroidered Chantilly lace over silk georgette designed by fellow Texan Michael Faircloth. She carried a purse by Judith Leiber.

Hillary and William "Bill" Clinton brought a new generation to the White House. Born after World War II and raised in the 1960s, they were a young power couple with a shared commitment to public service and politics. Bill saw Hillary as his greatest ally and appointed her chair of the President's Task Force on National Health Care Reform. She labored to create a health care system that would offer affordable coverage to all Americans, but many people thought her initiatives overstepped the proper role for a first lady. Her reform plans were rejected by Congress. More successful were her efforts on behalf of families worldwide. Her best-selling book *It Takes a Village* addressed how societies must come together to meet the needs of children.

Hillary was born in 1947 in Illinois and attended Wellesley College and Yale Law School, where she met fellow student Bill Clinton. After graduation she worked for the Children's Defense Fund and served as advisor to the House Judiciary Committee. She followed when Bill returned to his home state of Arkansas to pursue a career in politics, and they were married in 1975. Hillary worked as a lawyer while raising their daughter Chelsea.

President Clinton's second term in the White House was marred by controversy, but Hillary continued to work on domestic policy issues. In 2000 she became the first first lady to run for political office and was elected senator from New York. In 2008 she unsuccessfully challenged Barack Obama for the Democratic nomination for president. She later served as Obama's secretary of state from 2009 to 2013.

ABOVE: Bill and Hillary Clinton stand with designer Ralph Lauren in front of the Smithsonian's Star-Spangled Banner at the National Museum of American History.

RIGHT: Health care pamphlet. Mrs. Clinton worked with the president's staff on domestic policy issues from an office in the West Wing. Congress failed to pass her committee's proposed health care legislation. Some Americans vocally opposed a first lady holding such an overtly political position.

OPPOSITE: Sarah Phillips designed the violet-beaded lace sheath gown with iridescent blue velvet silk mousseline overskirt that Mrs. Clinton wore to the 1993 inaugural balls.

HEALTH SECURITY

A. B. JONES
123 45 6789

UNITED STATES OF AMERICA

HEALTH SECURITY
THE PRESIDENT'S HEALTH CARE PLAN

ABOVE TOP: Bumper sticker from campaign to be the Democratic Party's nominee in the 2008 presidential election.

ABOVE: Button from Hillary's successful run for the U.S. Senate. She became the junior senator from New York State on January 3, 2001, while still serving as first lady.

BARBARA PIERCE BUSH

The white-haired woman who entered the White House in 1989 was not dramatic or controversial. Instead, Barbara Bush's forthright, unthreatening, and friendly manner won her popularity. She was, as she put it, "everybody's grandmother." An advocate for literacy, she often read to children in schools and wrote *Millie's Book*, which offered "first dog" Millie's perspective on life in the White House. Profits from the book funded the Barbara Bush Foundation for Family Literacy. During the Gulf War, Barbara spoke to military audiences in encouragement and joined the president on a visit to American troops stationed in Saudi Arabia.

Born in 1925 and raised in Rye, New York, Barbara attended boarding school and at a dance met George H. W. Bush, a student at Phillips Academy in Andover, Massachusetts. Still teenagers, they became engaged just before he left to serve as a pilot in World War II. They were married in 1945. After the war, George attended Yale University. He eventually turned to public service and politics. Barbara was an asset to her husband through his years as a congressman, ambassador to the United Nations, CIA director, and vice president. She was a devoted mother to their six children. When their daughter Robin died of leukemia at age four, Barbara and George developed a deep compassion for all children and those in need.

After they left the White House in 1993, the Bushes settled in Houston, Texas. They spend summers with their children and grandchildren in Kennebunkport, Maine. Barbara, who remains active in many charitable organizations, proudly saw her son George W. Bush elected president in 2000.

ABOVE: President and Barbara Bush accompany General Norman Schwarzkopf and military personnel in Saudi Arabia on November 22, 1990.

CENTER RIGHT: Button from 1992 presidential campaign.

FAR RIGHT: In 1989 Mrs. Bush founded the Barbara Bush Foundation for Family Literacy and supported its projects with profits from *Millie's Book*, her 1990 "collaboration" with the family dog. The lighthearted story described a day in the White House from the perspective of Millie, the "first dog."

OPPOSITE: Mrs. Bush wore this royal-blue satin and velvet gown designed by Arnold Scassi to the 1989 inaugural balls.

Re-elect Barbara's Husband in '92

MILLIE'S BOOK

AS DICTATED TO BARBARA BUSH

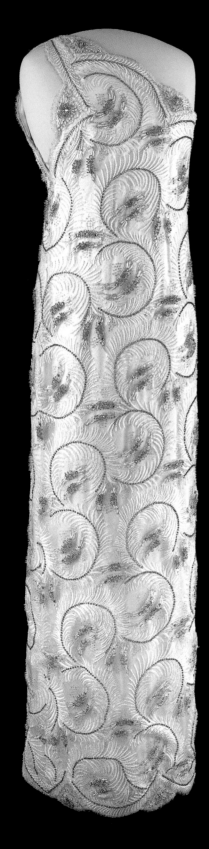
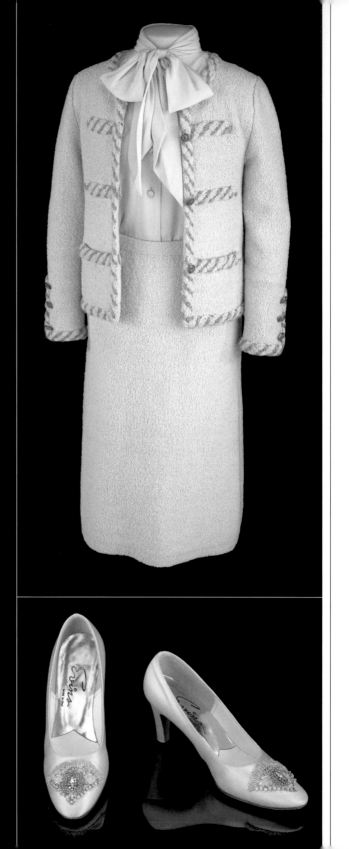

NANCY DAVIS REAGAN

Nancy Davis gave up a career as a Hollywood actress to marry actor Ronald "Ron" Reagan in 1951. The couple had two children together, and while Ron progressed from being the head of the Screen Actors Guild to governor of California, she volunteered for efforts benefiting war veterans, the elderly, and the handicapped. As first lady she continued to back those causes and also initiated an antidrug campaign with the now-familiar slogan "Just Say No." Nancy brought Hollywood glamour and diplomatic finesse to the White House. She countered the hard-line influence of some of the president's foreign policy advisors and encouraged Ron in his efforts to build a peaceful relationship with the Soviet Union. Nancy entertained foreign leaders at fifty-five state dinners, including one for Soviet leader Mikhail Gorbachev that provided a celebratory end to a Washington summit and the signing of the 1987 Intermediate-Range Nuclear Forces Treaty.

Raised in Chicago, Nancy majored in theater at Smith College in Massachusetts. After graduation she landed a role on Broadway. Eventually she moved to Hollywood, where she appeared in eleven films. In her last picture, *Hellcats of the Navy*, she costarred with her husband.

After an assassination attempt on her husband's life in 1981, Nancy's concerns for his safety and legacy prompted her to become more involved with White House scheduling and staffing decisions. She later published a memoir, *My Turn*, about her years in Washington. Ron died in 2004. Nancy lives in Bel Air, California, where she is involved with the Ronald Reagan Presidential Library.

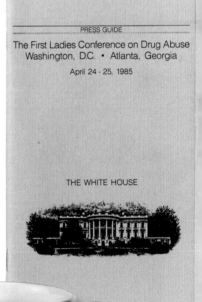

RIGHT: Press Guide. As part of her "Just Say No" campaign, Mrs. Reagan hosted a conference on drug abuse. First ladies from eighteen countries attended.

BELOW: Coffee cup and saucer from the Reagan White House china service. Although the 4,370-piece service in Nancy Reagan's signature red was acquired with private donations, its cost stirred controversy.

PRESS GUIDE

The First Ladies Conference on Drug Abuse
Washington, D.C. • Atlanta, Georgia

April 24 - 25, 1985

THE WHITE HOUSE

ABOVE: President and Nancy Reagan with Raisa and Mikhail Gorbachev at the White House on December 8, 1987.
OPPOSITE: Nancy Reagan chose this beaded one-shouldered gown by James Galanos for the 1981 inaugural balls. David Evins designed her beaded shoes (BOTTOM RIGHT). She wore a cream-colored Adolfo suit to the 1980 Republican National Convention (TOP RIGHT).

ROSALYNN SMITH CARTER

With Southern charm and intense focus, Rosalynn Carter, dubbed the "Steel Magnolia" by the press, further expanded the role of first lady. She represented her husband on an official trip to Latin America, where she discussed politics and issues with foreign leaders, much to the shock of some Americans. A full partner to her husband, Rosalynn believed in the president's agenda and worked hard to help him implement it. She even attended cabinet meetings and served as honorary chairperson on the President's Commission on Mental Health. Rosalynn also actively supported the Equal Rights Amendment. In her first fourteen months in the White House, she held twenty-two press conferences and hosted eighty-three official receptions.

Born in Plains, Georgia, in 1927, Rosalynn enrolled in college and in 1945 met Jimmy Carter, who was home from the U.S. Naval Academy. After their marriage the next year, Rosalynn followed Jimmy to various naval stations. They moved back to Plains to run the family peanut business, with Rosalynn managing accounts, after Jimmy's father died. Jimmy won a seat in the Georgia state senate in 1962 and was elected governor in 1970.

The Iranian Hostage Crisis that began in 1979 clouded Carter's presidency. While Jimmy focused on forging a resolution in Washington, Rosalynn took to the campaign trail, working vigorously for his re-election in 1980. Following his disappointing loss, they returned to Plains and dedicated themselves to public service. Rosalynn serves as chair of the Carter Center in Atlanta, which promotes human rights and peace worldwide.

LEFT: Thorton Utz's oil painting of Rosalynn Carter, daughter Amy, and family cat Misty Malarky Ying Yang is a replica of one that hung in President Jimmy Carter's office in the White House. BELOW: Button from 1980 presidential campaign.

TOP RIGHT: Rosalynn Carter and Betty Ford attended the National Women's Conference in Houston on November 19, 1977. They served as honorary co-chairs of a rally supporting the ERA. BOTTOM RIGHT: Breaking with tradition, the Carters walked down part of Pennsylvania Avenue during the inaugural parade on January 20, 1977. OPPOSITE: Mrs. Carter wore this gold-embroidered sleeveless coat over a gold-trimmed blue chiffon gown to the 1977 inaugural balls. She wore the same dress, designed by Mary Matise for Jimmae, to her husband's 1971 inaugural ball as governor of Georgia. The purse is by After Five.

ELIZABETH BLOOMER FORD

Candid, independent, and outspoken, Betty Ford broke many of the unwritten rules for first ladies. She may have been surprised to find herself in the White House after Richard Nixon's sudden resignation, but she was well prepared for the role.

Just a month after entering the White House, Betty broke with tradition and held a formal press conference to answer questions on politics, women's issues, abortion, and other controversial topics. After she was diagnosed with breast cancer, she openly discussed her mastectomy in the hopes of raising awareness of the disease. Unlike her husband Gerald, she supported a proposed Equal Rights Amendment to the Constitution. In a speech at the International Women's Year Conference in 1975, she declared, "I do not believe that being First Lady should prevent me from expressing my views....Why should my husband's job or yours prevent us from being ourselves?"

Elizabeth Bloomer was born in Chicago in 1918 and raised in Michigan. She attended the Bennington School of Dance, where she studied with choreographer Martha Graham. She married Gerald Ford in 1948, just two weeks before he was elected to Congress. During his twenty-five years in the House of Representatives, Betty worked as a volunteer and raised four children.

After the Fords left the White House in 1977, Betty sought treatment for a dependency on prescription painkillers and alcohol. With characteristic honesty, she shared her rehabilitation with the public. Before her death in 2011, she cofounded the Betty Ford Center to help others suffering from chemical dependency.

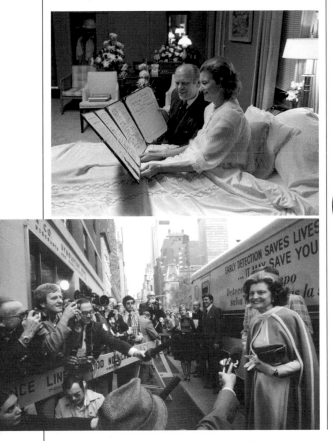

ERA
"Equality of rights under the law shall not be denied or abridged by the United States or by any State on account of sex."

BETTY'S HUSBAND FOR PRESIDENT IN '76

RATIFY ERA IN 1975

TOP RIGHT: Betty Ford supported the ERA during a trip to Florida in 1975.
CENTER: ERA and 1976 campaign buttons. Many people agreed with Mrs. Ford's support of the ERA and voted for her husband.
TOP LEFT: President and Mrs. Ford read a petition signed by every U.S. senator following her breast cancer surgery in 1974.
BOTTOM LEFT: Mrs. Ford answers questions prior to touring the Guttman Institute for Early Detection of Breast Cancer in New York in 1975.
OPPOSITE: Betty Ford wore this pale-green sequined chiffon gown designed by Frankie Welch to state dinners at the White House.

At her birth in 1912, Thelma Ryan's father nicknamed her "Pat." She used that name throughout her life. Both of her parents died by the time Pat was eighteen years old. She worked her way through the University of Southern California and eventually became a high school teacher in Whittier, the hometown of Richard Nixon. They were married in 1940, and Pat took a government job while Richard served in the Navy and was later elected to Congress. While Richard served as vice president in Eisenhower's administration, Pat raised their two daughters and accompanied her husband on scores of diplomatic visits. She proved to be a tireless campaigner during Richard's unsuccessful 1960 bid for the presidency and again during his victorious 1968 presidential campaign.

RIGHT: Button from 1960 presidential campaign. Mrs. Nixon became the first candidate's wife to "run" for first lady during the campaign's "Pat for First Lady" week in October.

In the White House, Pat advocated volunteerism and used the position of first lady to further her cause. Pat encouraged her husband to nominate a woman to the Supreme Court and was the first first lady to endorse the Equal Rights Amendment. She also added five hundred paintings and antiques to the White House collection. The early 1970s were a turbulent time for the Nixons and the country, with opposition growing to the war in Vietnam and escalating racial and social unrest at home. The Watergate scandal resulted in the president's resignation from office in 1974.

It was a sad ending for a dignified woman who had traveled to diplomatic summits in China and the Soviet Union, brought relief to earthquake victims in Peru, and visited a combat zone in Vietnam. Pat made few public appearances after leaving the White House. She died in 1993.

ABOVE: Pat Nixon made many overseas visits on behalf of her husband, including a trip to Liberia in 1972. Dressed in a traditional garment and turban, she joined dancers at the presidential palace.
LEFT: Invitation to the wedding of Tricia Nixon to Edward Cox on June 12, 1971. Held in the Rose Garden, it was the sixteenth wedding ceremony to take place at the White House.
OPPOSITE: Mrs. Nixon's 1969 inaugural ball gown featured a silk satin jacket embroidered in gold and silver and encrusted with Austrian crystals. The gown and bolero jacket were designed by Karen Stark for Harvey Berin; the matching shoes are by Herbert Levine.

Pat FOR FIRST LADY

The President and Mrs. Nixon request the honor of your presence at the marriage of their daughter Patricia to Mr. Edward Finch Cox on Saturday, the twelfth of June one thousand nine hundred and seventy-one at four o'clock in the afternoon The White House

CLAUDIA TAYLOR JOHNSON

When Claudia Taylor was a child in Texas, everyone called her "Lady Bird," and the nickname stuck. Entering the White House after the tragic assassination of John Kennedy, she did her best to comfort a grieving nation. She promoted her husband's vision of a Great Society by creating a First Lady's Committee for a More Beautiful Capital, a program that aimed to clean up poverty-stricken neighborhoods in Washington, D.C., and improve the quality of life for those who lived in them. The first lady ultimately expanded the program to other areas across the nation and supported legislation promoting the Highway Beautification Act, also known as Lady Bird's Bill. In addition, she became involved in Head Start, a preschool program for underprivileged children.

Raised in a prosperous Texas family, Lady Bird earned two bachelor's degrees from the University of Texas at Austin. In 1934 she met and married Lyndon Johnson. Through his years as a congressman and senator, World War II, and his severe heart attack in 1955, she kept his work and family afloat. During Lyndon's 1964 presidential campaign, she made a difficult four-day journey of 1,628 miles on a train called the "Lady Bird Special" to garner support for her husband in the South.

Lyndon did not run for re-election in 1968, and the Johnsons retired to their ranch in Texas, where the former president died in 1973. Lady Bird devoted her time to environmental causes and to the LBJ Presidential Library. In 1988 she became the first first lady to receive a Congressional Gold Medal. She died in 2007.

ABOVE: Lady Bird Johnson plants pansies, one of her many beautification projects in DC in hopes of making the capital a model for other urban areas.

RIGHT: This brooch, a gift to Mrs. Johnson in celebration of the gem and mineral wealth of the United States, contains stones from each of the fifty states.

ABOVE: In a pamphlet of her speeches published during the 1964 presidential campaign, the first lady encouraged women to become engaged with government and work for better communities.
OPPOSITE: Mrs. Johnson wore this ensemble of sable-trimmed coat and yellow satin gown designed by John Moore to the 1965 inaugural balls.

TOP: Toy train table decoration and an invitation (CENTER LEFT) for a brunch honoring Mrs. Johnson's 1964 campaign trip aboard the "Lady Bird Special." On the whistle-stop tour from Washington to New Orleans, the first lady spoke to sometimes-hostile crowds angered by the president's support of the 1964 Civil Rights Act. It was the first time a first lady made   a whistle-stop tour by herself. The yellow postcard (CENTER RIGHT) announces the trip.
BOTTOM LEFT: Mrs. Johnson waves from the "Lady Bird Special" train during the 1964 election.

TOP: Satin-covered box of wedding cake from Luci Johnson's marriage to Patrick Nugent on August 6, 1966. President and Mrs. Johnson hosted the reception at the White House.

ABOVE: Lady Bird Johnson's special affection for wildflowers is represented in her White House china service. "Beautification"—a combination of environmentalism, conservation, urban renewal, and community activism—became her signature program during her years as first lady.

RIGHT: Invitation to the wedding of Lynda Johnson to Charles Robb in the East Room of the White House on December 9, 1967.

The President and Mrs. Johnson
request the honour of your presence
at the marriage of their daughter
Lynda Bird
to
Charles Spittal Robb
Captain, United States Marine Corps
on Saturday, the ninth of December
one thousand nine hundred and sixty-seven
at four o'clock in the afternoon
The White House

JACQUELINE BOUVIER KENNEDY

Jacqueline Kennedy came from a privileged background and was dazzlingly elegant, well read, and interested in art and culture. She stole the show when she and President Kennedy made a diplomatic trip to France in 1961. He joked, "I am the man who accompanied Jacqueline Kennedy to Paris, and I have enjoyed it."

Jackie was born in 1929 and raised in New York City. She was educated at Vassar College and George Washington University. After graduation, she ventured into journalism, landing a job as the "Inquiring Camera Girl" at the *Washington Times–Herald*. That was how she met John "Jack" Kennedy, a young senator from Massachusetts. They were married in 1953. Jack's successful presidential campaign in 1960 brought a vibrant young family to the White House. The antics of three-year-old Caroline and infant John Jr. fascinated the public, and the press adored Jackie in her designer suits and pillbox hats. Jackie invited poets, artists, and musicians to the White House, and she oversaw the complete restoration of the mansion. Her televised tour of the newly decorated White House won her an honorary Emmy award.

President Kennedy's assassination in 1963 brought an end to an ideal time at the White House. Images of the happy first family were replaced by scenes of the grief-stricken yet dignified widow, who tried to maintain a private life for herself and her children. Jackie later worked to establish the John F. Kennedy Library in Boston as a way to preserve her husband's legacy. In 1975 she married Greek businessman Aristotle Onassis. She moved to New York City and enjoyed a successful career in publishing before her death from cancer in 1994.

ABOVE: Jacqueline Kennedy during the filming of a CBS News special program called *A Tour of the White House with Mrs. John F. Kennedy*, which aired on January 15, 1962.

LEFT: The newly sworn-in president and first lady leave the White House on January 20, 1961, for a tour of the inaugural balls.

OPPOSITE: Jackie Kennedy wore this off-white sleeveless gown of silk chiffon over *peau d'ange* to the 1961 inaugural balls. The strapless bodice under the chiffon covering is encrusted with brilliants and embroidered with silver thread. Ethel Frankau of Bergdorf Custom Salon designed the dress and matching cape based on sketches and suggestions from Mrs. Kennedy.

TOP LEFT: Entertainment program from the 1963 state dinner for the president of India. Believing "everything in the White House should be the best," Jackie Kennedy invited distinguished artists to perform there.

ABOVE: The first lady christens the USS *Lafayette* in 1962.

CENTER LEFT: Mrs. Kennedy often wore a costume pearl necklace.

LEFT: John Jr., Jackie, Caroline, and John Kennedy spend time at Hyannis Port on Cape Cod, Massachusetts, in August 1962.

OPPOSITE LEFT: Deemed a fashion icon, Jackie Kennedy consistently topped best-dressed lists. Oleg Cassini designed this satin evening gown. "The Jackie Look" became popular, and copies of the first lady's clothes were sold in stores across the country.

OPPOSITE RIGHT: For the administration's state dinner for Tunisian president Habib Bourguibailk in 1961, Jackie Kennedy wore this yellow silk evening gown designed by Oleg Cassini.

MAMIE DOUD EISENHOWER

With her distinctive bangs, her love of anything pink, and her charm and sparkle, Mamie Eisenhower won the affection of American voters. They may have "liked Ike," but they loved Mamie. An army wife accustomed to frequent moves and unfamiliar social situations, Mamie truly enjoyed the role of first lady. She attracted women to politics and brought them to the polls. By the 1950s women were casting ballots in equal numbers to men, and the Eisenhower campaign used Mamie to appeal to female voters by issuing "Mamie for First Lady" buttons.

Born in Boone, Iowa, Mamie Doud moved to Colorado at an early age. Attractive and indulged, Mamie hardly seemed the type to marry a military man, but once she wed Dwight ("Ike") Eisenhower, a graduate of West Point, she followed him to posts in the Panama Canal Zone, France, and the Philippines.

Ike's fame as a general in World War II led both Republicans and Democrats to court him for the presidency in 1952. He ran on the Republican ticket and won in a landslide victory. With the war years behind them, Americans enjoyed peace and prosperity. Mamie hosted large-scale social events at the White House, and the Eisenhowers entertained heads of state, diplomats, and foreign leaders. Their son and grandchildren were also frequent visitors. Mamie's personal style of glamour mixed with folksiness added to her public appeal and reinforced the optimism of the era.

The Eisenhowers retired to a home they built in Gettysburg, Pennsylvania, in 1961. After Ike's death the next year, Mamie lived there, still much loved and respected, until her own death in 1979.

MARTYN GREEN

An evening of music
from "Iolanthe" and "The Mikado"
by Gilbert and Sullivan

SHIRLEY JONES and JACK CASSIDY

Songs of
Victor Herbert
and
Rodgers and Hammerstein

Tuesday, January 29, 1957
THE WHITE HOUSE

LEFT: Program from a 1957 musicale at the Eisenhower White House that featured selections by Gilbert and Sullivan as well as Rodgers and Hammerstein.
BELOW: Button from 1952 presidential election. Mamie Eisenhower was popular on the campaign trail.

MAMIE FOR **FIRST LADY**

RIGHT: Mrs. Eisenhower ordered a set of service plates to complement the still-new Truman china service in the White House.

ABOVE: Clad in bathrobes, Mamie and Dwight Eisenhower wave from their campaign train in Salisbury, North Carolina, on September 27, 1952.
OPPOSITE: Mrs. Eisenhower wore this rhinestone embellished pink *peau de soie* gown designed by Nettie Rosenstein to the 1953 inaugural balls. "Mamie pink" became a fashion trend.

ELIZABETH WALLACE TRUMAN

Elizabeth "Bess" Truman, a Missouri girl with strong opinions, married fellow Missourian Harry Truman in 1919 after his service in World War I. As Harry grew increasingly active in politics, Bess became a partner in his endeavors, traveling, campaigning, and when he was elected to the U.S. Senate, moving their close-knit family to Washington. There, "the Boss," as Harry often called her, joined his office as a paid staff member. Harry's position on a special committee on defense spending earned him the vice-presidential spot on the 1944 ticket with Franklin Roosevelt. The president's sudden death in 1945 catapulted Harry to the White House in the midst of World War II and put Bess in the very public—and very unwelcome—role of first lady.

While Harry grappled with the huge task of bringing the war to an end, which included the controversial decision to drop atomic bombs on two Japanese cities, Bess recoiled from the lack of privacy in the White House. She kept a limited social calendar, met only with the most traditional charities, and held no press conferences. She might not have had much to say to reporters, but she did talk to the president. He later recalled their closeness, calling her his "chief advisor" and claiming she was "a full partner in all my transactions—politically and otherwise."

The Trumans moved to Independence, Missouri, in 1953. Harry died in 1972, and Bess passed away ten years later. Their daughter Margaret wrote several books about her famous parents as well as a series of popular mysteries set in Washington, D.C.

ABOVE: Bess Truman meets with a delegation of Girl Scouts. They presented a glass paperweight to thank her for her service as their organization's honorary president since 1945. Two unidentified Girl Scout leaders look on as (left to right) Susan Schneider, 11; Loretta Gallegos, 8; Joanna Rodman, 8; and Marian East, 16, meet the first lady.

ABOVE: Pieces from the White House china service that Bess and Harry Truman ordered. The celadon-green border matched the walls of the newly redecorated State Dining Room. The Trumans lived across the street at Blair House from 1948 to 1952 during the White House renovation.

OPPOSITE: Mrs. Truman wore this silver lamé and gray satin gown to an inaugural reception held at the National Gallery of Art in 1949.

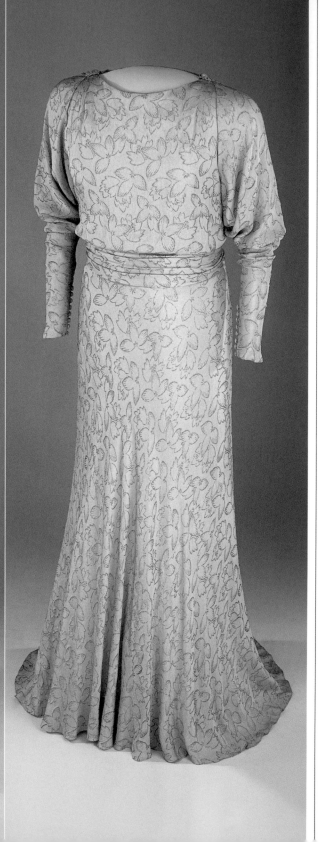

ANNA ELEANOR ROOSEVELT

Eleanor Roosevelt was a new kind of first lady. She was born into political elite society (Teddy Roosevelt was her uncle), yet she experienced great loss as a child. Both of her parents died before she was ten, and she grew up to be a strong advocate for the underprivileged. As a young woman, Eleanor offered educational programs to the poor at New York's Rivington Street Settlement House and volunteered for the Red Cross during World War I.

In 1905 she wed her fifth cousin, Franklin Delano Roosevelt, and later gave birth to six children. Through their marriage, Eleanor became a politician's wife, a Washington insider, and when Franklin was stricken with polio, a caregiver. Eleanor compensated for her husband's physical limitations by putting herself in the political spotlight, supporting him during his successful run for governor of New York in 1928 and helping him campaign for the presidency in 1932. Franklin served four terms in office, making Eleanor the longest serving first lady.

Eleanor connected with Americans by holding press conferences, giving lectures, and traveling throughout the United States and abroad. Her opinions appeared in a daily syndicated newspaper column called "My Day." To provide Americans with needed reassurance during World War II, Eleanor visited families on the home front and troops stationed abroad.

After Franklin's death in 1945, Eleanor was appointed special delegate to the United Nations. In 1961 President John F. Kennedy appointed her chair of his Commission on the Status of Women. Eleanor died in 1962 at the age of seventy-eight.

ABOVE: Eleanor Roosevelt tours a coal mine with union officials in 1935.

TOP RIGHT: Mrs. Roosevelt's horn-rimmed sunglasses.

FAR RIGHT: She wore this pink rayon crepe gown to an inaugural reception in 1945. The use of rayon rather than silk may have been a war conservation measure, since silk was used for parachutes.

CENTER: While a delegate to the United Nations, Eleanor Roosevelt wore this mink coat with her monogram embroidered in the lining. She promoted ready-to-wear clothing but cautioned against buying goods made in sweatshops.

OPPOSITE: Sally Milgrim designed this silk crepe evening gown for the 1933 inaugural ball. The first lady wore it without the detachable sleeves.

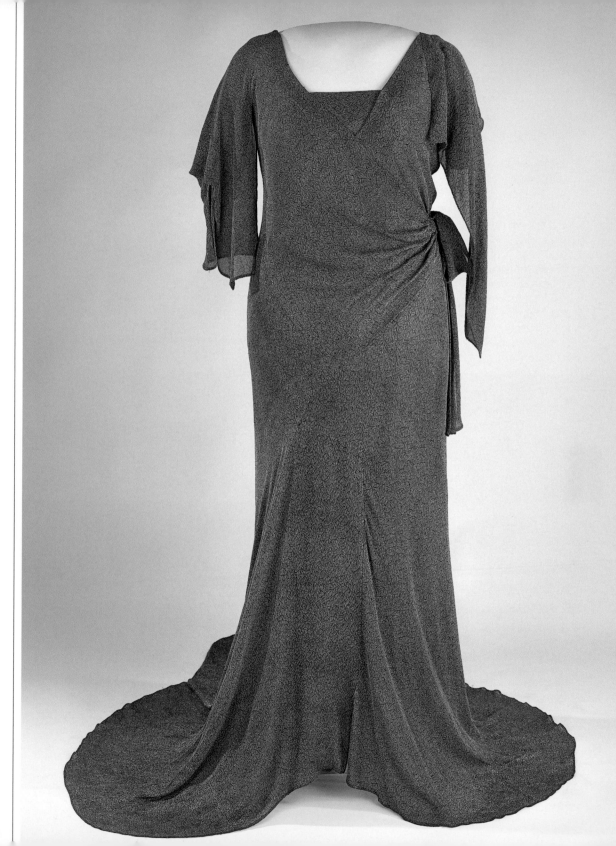

LOU HENRY HOOVER

Possessing a love of foreign languages and adventure, Lou Henry Hoover was the first woman at Stanford University to graduate in the "man's field" of geology. An extraordinary role model for twentieth-century women, she advocated for the Girl Scouts of America, believing girls could gain self-reliance and self-esteem through social service and volunteerism.

Lou was also the first wife of a president to speak on the radio, and she addressed national audiences on numerous occasions. During the Great Depression she stressed charitable giving in her speeches. The Hoovers were much criticized for holding lavish events at the White House during those difficult years. Unknown to the press or public, they paid some of the White House staff with their own funds and helped many people in need.

Born in Waterloo, Iowa, in 1874, Lou moved to California ten years later. At Stanford she met Herbert Hoover, who was studying to be a mining engineer. They married in 1899, just before they left for China, where Herbert oversaw mining operations. While in Tientsin (now spelled Tianjin), the Hoovers and other foreign nationals were held under siege during the violent Boxer Rebellion.

Herbert distinguished himself as an administrator of emergency relief during World War I, and he was appointed secretary of commerce in 1921. Lou had the misfortune to become first lady just before the stock market crash of 1929. Considered ineffective during the nation's suffering, Herbert lost the 1932 election, and the family returned to Palo Alto, California. Lou's private generosity during the Depression was never revealed or acknowledged until after her death in 1944.

RIGHT: A costume-jewelry brooch fastens at the waist of this floral-patterned day dress. When Mrs. Hoover became first lady in 1929, she was one of the "best-dressed women in official life." She always wore American-made clothes, and she made a point of wearing cotton dresses to promote the cotton textile industry.
ABOVE: Lou Hoover posed for a photograph wearing the evening gown (OPPOSITE) and these lorgnette glasses and beaded chain (ABOVE LEFT).
OPPOSITE: Lou Hoover selected this silk crepe evening gown for the closing banquet of a Girl Scout convention. She not only served as national president of the Girl Scouts before and after being first lady, but she was also honorary president during her years in the White House.

GRACE GOODHUE COOLIDGE

Unlike her husband "Silent Cal," Grace Coolidge was outgoing and sociable. Grace loved being outdoors, had many pets (including Rebecca the raccoon), and willingly posed for photographs, although she did not grant interviews. Her high visibility counterbalanced the dour image of her husband and popularized the Coolidge White House.

Grace grew up in Burlington and graduated from the University of Vermont in 1902. She moved to Northampton, Massachusetts, where she taught at the Clarke School of the Deaf and met Calvin Coolidge on local church-sponsored outings. After their marriage in 1905, the couple lived modestly as Calvin rose from small-town lawyer to governor. Her involvement in the community surely aided in the success of her serious, reserved husband. She was also a devoted mother to their two sons. Despite the death of Cal, her sixteen-year-old son, during her tenure as first lady, Grace fulfilled her social duties and did not let the family's grief overshadow the concerns of the nation.

Although their personalities seemed mismatched, Grace and Silent Cal were a happy couple. After his presidency, they returned to their home in Northampton and lived there until Calvin's death in 1933. Later in life, Grace served as a trustee of the Clarke School and occasionally enjoyed watching the Red Sox play baseball at Fenway Park in Boston. She lent her name to several causes during World War II, including the WAVES (Women Accepted for Voluntary Emergency Service). Grace never visited the White House, but she wrote many supportive letters to her successors as first lady before her death in 1957.

ABOVE: Grace Coolidge enjoyed needlework. She made this needlepoint handbag and even crocheted a spread for the Lincoln bed in the White House.

RIGHT: Mrs. Coolidge's hand mirror.

OPPOSITE: Mrs. Coolidge gave this blue satin flapper-style evening gown trimmed with dark blue sequins and gold glass beads to Maggie Rogers, her White House maid. It was likely shortened to be worn by Maggie's daughter Lillian. American women appreciated the first lady's sense of fashion and her more sedate versions of the 1920s flapper style. Grace Coolidge liked to go on shopping trips, and the president enjoyed selecting dresses and hats for her.

TOP LEFT: Grace Coolidge's Pi Beta Phi sorority pin. She was a founding member of the University of Vermont chapter and proudly wore her pin long after graduating in 1902.

TOP RIGHT: Museum visitors preferred this "Coolidge red" chiffon velvet dress and its matching velvet shoes with rhinestone trim (BOTTOM RIGHT) to the white evening gown that the first lady originally sent for the Smithsonian's collection.

BOTTOM LEFT: Brown chiffon and lace dress trimmed with metallic thread and a brown velvet bow.

OPPOSITE: Evening dress made of velvet-trimmed black-and-gold metallic lace over a gold lamé underdress.

The daughter of a strong-willed and successful businessman in Ohio, Florence Kling grew up with many of her father's traits. Self-reliant and shrewd, she rebounded from a bad early marriage and earned a living by giving music lessons. She met and married Warren Harding, a young newspaperman who bought the *Marion Daily Star* and established her as head of the circulation department. Florence used her natural business skills to turn the newspaper into a profitable enterprise.

The newspaper helped Warren enter local politics, and he eventually was elected a U.S. senator. Just as she had managed the *Star*, Florence ran her husband's political career. When he became a presidential nominee in 1920, she helped Warren run a masterful "front porch" campaign from their home in Marion, Ohio. She understood the value of creating a public image, which proved vital to her husband's political success.

The first woman to vote for her husband in a presidential election, Florence supported women's causes and achievements as first lady and also took an active concern in veterans' affairs. Her "management style," which had helped Warren attain the presidency, was less effective once he was in office. Some of his closest advisors were implicated in wrongdoing that could have been the president's demise, but Warren, who had been in poor health, died unexpectedly while on a cross-country tour in 1923 before details of corruption came to light. Florence was much maligned after her husband's death. She refused to permit an autopsy, which led to speculations she had murdered him. Florence died just a year later in 1924.

ABOVE: Pinning a flower on actor Al Jolson's lapel during a campaign appearance by the "Harding-Coolidge Theatrical League," Florence Harding acted as one of her husband's campaign managers and was skilled at arranging photo opportunities such as this one.
RIGHT: Mrs. Harding's evening gown, designed by Harry Collins, features pearlized sequins on tulle and rhinestone-trimmed blue velvet ribbon.

EDITH BOLLING GALT WILSON

On her deathbed, Woodrow Wilson's wife Ellen encouraged him to marry again—and he did, just over a year after her death. Edith Bolling was born and raised in rural Virginia and married a prosperous businessman, Norman Galt, in 1896. Twelve years later she was a childless widow living in the nation's capital. She was also the savvy manager of her late husband's business and a woman of great beauty and charm when the lonely widowed president met her. They were married in December 1915.

Edith did not have a political background, but she was smart and had her husband's interests at heart. With the United States involved in World War I for much of her tenure in the White House, Edith assisted her husband with his correspondence and even learned to decode military and diplomatic messages. The strain of the war caught up with the president in 1919 when, after a monumental effort to win support for the Treaty of Versailles and the establishment of the League of Nations, he was partially paralyzed by a stroke. Concerned for her husband's health, Edith stepped in. She strictly controlled access to the president, determined what issues would and would not receive his attention, and transmitted his instructions to government officials. The first lady referred to her temporary role as a "stewardship," but many accused her of making it a "regency" and attempting to single-handedly gain control. She strongly defended her actions, noting that her intervention was critical to her husband's survival. Woodrow died three years after leaving the White House, but Edith continued to live in Washington for four more decades.

TOP LEFT: Edith Wilson wore this homemade Red Cross hat while volunteering during World War I.
CENTER LEFT: The people of Paris presented this brooch to Mrs. Wilson when she accompanied her husband to peace treaty negotiations in 1919. It was designed by René Lalique and features glass doves perch on diamond-studded gold laurel sprays.
BOTTOM LEFT: Green satin pumps.

ABOVE: Pansy-patterned fan.
RIGHT: For a private dinner party held at the White House in 1915, Edith Wilson selected this black charmeuse satin evening dress from the House of Worth in Paris.

ELLEN AXSON WILSON

Although she did not look forward to being first lady, the quiet, artistic, and socially conscious Ellen Wilson made the White House welcoming in a low-key way. No inaugural ball marked the beginning of Woodrow Wilson's term, and dinner parties were sedate affairs, yet Ellen was considered an important political asset to her husband. After visiting the squalid alleys only blocks from the U.S. Capitol, she became an advocate for housing reform, using her position to lobby Congress to improve the quality of life for the city's impoverished African American community. She also planted the now-famous White House Rose Garden and redecorated the mansion's private quarters with handicrafts made by Appalachian women, whose efforts she publicly recognized.

The daughter of a Presbyterian minister, Ellen Axson grew up in Rome, Georgia. She married Woodrow Wilson in 1885 and followed him north to Bryn Mawr College in Pennsylvania, where he started his teaching career. The couple had three daughters and eventually moved to Princeton, New Jersey, where Woodrow became president of the university. When he was elected governor of New Jersey, Ellen had to step into a public role. The White House, however, was a much bigger arena. In her few private hours, Ellen managed to paint in a studio she had installed in the Executive Mansion.

On August 6, 1914, Ellen died of a kidney ailment called Bright's disease. Just before she passed away, the U.S. Congress passed a slum reform bill that is historically referred to as the Ellen Wilson Bill.

ABOVE: A talented painter who had studied at the Art Students League in New York, Ellen Wilson exhibited, and even sold, some of her landscapes while she served as first lady. She painted this view of Cornish, New Hampshire, in 1913.
RIGHT: Brocade velvet gown worn by Mrs. Wilson.

HELEN HERRON TAFT

Helen "Nellie" Herron had her eye on the White House even before she married William Howard Taft. The well-educated and ambitious Ohio native had visited the President's Mansion as a teenager. Decades later, the energetic and independent first lady hosted dazzling White House receptions of her own and in 1912 made a lasting gift to the city of Washington, D.C.— arranging for the gift and planting of the thousands of Japanese cherry trees that circle the Tidal Basin.

With her love of politics, Nellie supported and nurtured her husband's career. When he took the post of U.S. governor to the Philippines in 1900, she moved their three children across the world and embraced the unfamiliar culture with diplomacy and tact. William's appointment as secretary of war in 1904 put him in line for a chance at the presidency. His victory in 1908 pleased Nellie more than it did William, who truly longed to be a Supreme Court justice.

Nellie was the first first lady to ride beside her husband to the White House after the swearing-in ceremony at the Capitol. This break with tradition signaled her active role in her husband's career. Only two months into his term, however, she suffered a stroke. Nellie began entertaining again in 1910 on a smaller scale, and in 1911 she hosted a garden party for several thousand guests in honor of her and William's silver wedding anniversary.

William attained his dream job when he was appointed chief justice of the Supreme Court later by President Harding in 1921. Nellie continued to play a role in Washington society, even after William's death in 1930. She passed away in 1943.

LEFT: Created by Frances Smith Company, Mrs. Taft's 1909 inaugural ball gown is made of white silk chiffon appliquéd with floral embroideries in metallic thread and trimmed with rhinestones and beads. The fabric and embroidery have become discolored, and much of the skirt was replaced in a 1940s conservation effort.

ABOVE LEFT: Helen Taft's green satin Manchu-style coat is embroidered with spring and summer symbols of goldfish and lotus flowers, but it is lined with fleece. The fur trim was probably added as a custom order.
ABOVE RIGHT: Mrs. Taft's inaugural ball gown featured a flowing train.
RIGHT: This silver lorgnette belonged to Helen Taft.

How could anyone have the energy to keep up with the robust Theodore Roosevelt? Edith Carow seemed unfazed. They had known each other as children growing up in New York City, where their families were friendly. They also spent time together at the Roosevelts' home in Oyster Bay, Long Island. When Theodore left to attend Harvard University, he and Edith drifted apart. They were reunited and married after Theodore's first wife died. Edith proved to be a calm and controlled counterpoint to Teddy's boisterous manner and large presence. Their lively family included five children plus Teddy's daughter Alice from his first marriage. After Teddy suddenly became president on the death of William McKinley, the family piled into the White House with various pets and prized possessions.

It was fun and hectic. The antics of Theodore Jr., Kermit, Ethel, Archibald, and Quentin captivated the press and the public, as did the sometimes scandalous behavior of the rebellious "Princess Alice."

Edith made every attempt to rein in the family while also presenting them in their best light. Her social secretary released posed photographs of the Roosevelt family for publication in approved newspapers and magazines. By managing her public image, Edith set a precedent that future first ladies followed. She also exerted the same control over Washington society. The first lady re-established the White House as the center of official social life and introduced a new formality that was intended to reinforce respect for the presidency.

After Theodore died in 1919, Edith remained at Sagamore Hill, their family home in Oyster Bay, until her death in 1948.

ABOVE: Plate from the Roosevelt White House china. The Wedgwood service was the first to incorporate the great seal of the United States in color as a part of the design.
OPPOSITE: Edith Roosevelt's 1905 inaugural ball gown featured a design of plumes and birds woven in gold thread. The skirt was altered and the original bodice was removed before the dress was donated to the Smithsonian.

ABOVE: Paint set used by Archie Roosevelt, son of Edith and Theodore Roosevelt, around 1903.
RIGHT: Silk calendar for 1904. To control press interest in her family, the first lady instructed her social secretary to release posed photographs for publication in newspapers and magazines. Commercial products depicting the first family were also available to an admiring public.

IDA SAXTON McKINLEY

Ida Saxton's youth held much promise. She was from a prominent family in Canton, Ohio, who saw to her education and sent her to Europe on a Grand Tour. Her open-minded father even allowed her to work in his bank as a cashier. There, beautiful Ida met her future husband, Major William McKinley, who was just beginning his law career. They were married and soon started a family, but after the birth of their daughter, who died at age four, Ida began to experience epileptic seizures that left her housebound. Doted on by her husband, who was elected a U.S. congressman and then governor of Ohio, Ida largely kept out of the public eye.

She made just a few appearances as part of McKinley's "front porch" presidential campaign but, despite her illness, Ida was determined to fulfill her role as first lady. Beautifully dressed, she gripped a floral bouquet at social functions so she would not have to shake hands with guests. When a seizure came on, the president placed a handkerchief over her face until it passed. Guests did not reveal the first lady's condition, and discrete newspapers, to which Ida was always gracious and available, did not report the extent of the first lady's ill health.

William McKinley was shot by an anarchist on September 6, 1901, while attending the Pan-American Exposition in Buffalo, New York. As he collapsed, his first words were filled with worry for his wife. Amazingly, Ida rallied during the eight days her husband lay dying, and she accompanied his coffin to Washington. She also attended his funeral. In mourning, Ida moved back to Ohio to live with her sister. She died in 1907.

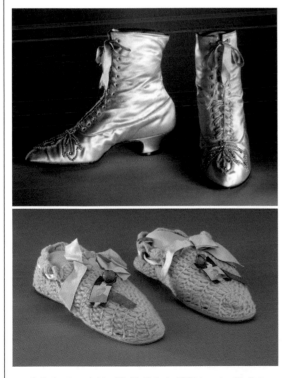

ABOVE: President McKinley had served a few months of his second term when he was assassinated in 1901. Sheet music mourning his death takes as its title his last words: "Goodbye to all, goodbye."

TOP: Satin boots matching Ida McKinley's 1901 inaugural ball gown.
BOTTOM: Mrs. McKinley crocheted slippers for charity. She made this pair for a "Puritan Fair" held at the First Congregational Church in Springfield, Massachusetts.

RIGHT: Dance card from the 1901 inaugural ball held at the Pension Building.
OPPOSITE: Ida McKinley wore this white satin gown to the inaugural ball in 1901.

CAROLINE SCOTT HARRISON

Daughter of a Presbyterian minister who founded the Oxford Female Institute in Ohio, Caroline Harrison possessed many talents. As first lady she used her influence to work for charities, such as the Johns Hopkins Medical School in Baltimore, but her generosity was not without "strings." Prior to raising funds for the facility, she insisted women be admitted—and the school agreed. She took an avid interest in history, becoming president general of the Daughters of the American Revolution and establishing the White House china collection. A skilled china painter, Carrie designed the corn and goldenrod pattern on the settings used during her husband's administration.

Carrie Scott met Benjamin Harrison when they were teenagers. Benjamin established a law practice in Indiana, and their lives centered on family, church, and community, with a brief interruption during the Civil War. When Benjamin was elected to the U.S. Senate, they relocated to Washington for a short period, but illness kept Carrie out of the limelight. Still, when her husband was elected president in 1888, she rallied and moved with her extended family, including that of her daughter Mary Harrison McKee, into cramped quarters at the White House. Her plans to renovate the mansion completely were not approved by Congress, so she modernized the building, on a very limited budget, to accommodate her needs. Carrie tried to fulfill her social obligations as first lady, but her health eventually gave out. She died of tuberculosis in 1892. Her daughter Mary took over the responsibilities of hostess for the remaining months of the president's term.

ABOVE: Mrs. Maria Ester Guzman of Nicaragua received this hand-painted favor at a White House dinner on April 7, 1891.

TOP RIGHT: The pattern that rims the Harrison White House china combines corn and goldenrod, the president's favorite flower. Forty-four stars decorate the interior rim and represent the number of states in the Union at the time. The first lady's interest in china led her to inventory the pieces from earlier services, locate missing pieces, and establish the White House china collection.

OPPOSITE: Caroline Harrison's burgundy velvet and gray satin evening gown is embroidered in a floral design with gray pearls and steel beads.

RIGHT: Following the administration's "America first" policy, Mrs. Harrison's 1889 inaugural ball gown was crafted of silk made in the U.S.

FRANCES FOLSOM CLEVELAND

Frances Folsom Cleveland was a sensation. At the age of twenty-one, the beautiful bride of forty-eight-year-old President Grover Cleveland stole the hearts of Americans. Their White House wedding—the first of a president held in the Executive Mansion—occurred in 1886. Charming and unaffected, the new Mrs. Cleveland hosted two receptions a week, with one held on Saturdays to accommodate working women.

Frances had the unusual fortune to be first lady twice; her husband was the only man to serve two nonconsecutive terms as president. When the couple returned to Washington for the second term in 1893, Frances, now a mother of one with another child on the way, slipped into the familiar role of first lady with effortless style.

She was born in Buffalo, New York, where her father, Oscar Folsom, became a friend and law partner of Grover Cleveland. After Folsom's death, Grover settled his partner's estate and served as an unofficial uncle to "Frank," as her family called her. Grover proposed to her after she graduated from Wells College. Their unexpected marriage and her popularity inspired advertisers to exploit the first lady's image, using her face on everything from pill boxes to playing cards. Incensed at the invasion of privacy, the president supported a bill restricting the commercial use of celebrities' likenesses without their permission. The bill did not pass.

The family settled in Princeton, New Jersey, after Grover left the White House. He died in 1908. Frances eventually remarried and lived to be eighty-three.

ABOVE: Frances Cleveland pictured in her wedding gown, which she wore again at a state reception on June 15 and a public reception on June 18, 1886. She had the dress altered to an evening gown style for these occasions.

TOP RIGHT: An advertising card for the Merrick Thread Company capitalized on the popularity of the newly married couple.

OPPOSITE: Frances Cleveland wore this silk evening gown with fur-edged hem and black satin-and-jet trim during her husband's second administration.

RIGHT: Mrs. Cleveland chose this satin gown for her White House wedding in 1886.

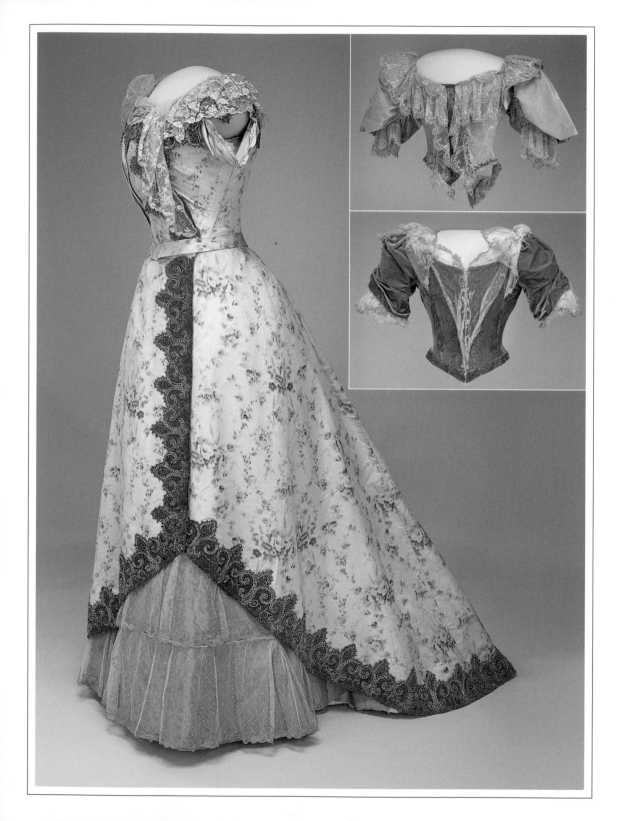

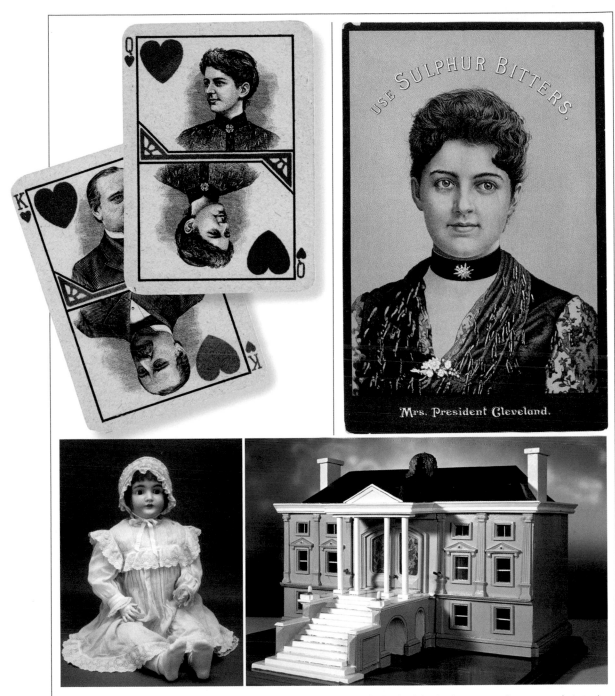

TOP: Playing cards and an advertising card featuring Frances Cleveland. Public fascination led to her image appearing on more photographs, souvenirs, and advertising paraphernalia than any other first lady in the nineteenth century.

BOTTOM LEFT: Esther Cleveland's doll. BOTTOM RIGHT: A White House gardener built this dollhouse for the Cleveland children around 1896.

OPPOSITE: Mrs. Cleveland's floral chine skirt has three coordinating bodices. The peach velvet bodice was probably made around 1895 by the House of Doucet in Paris. The floral bodice was later fashioned from the skirt's fabric. Baltimore dressmaker Lottie M. Barton created the green velvet bodice.

LUCRETIA RUDOLPH GARFIELD

First Lady: 1881

Four months into his presidential term, James Garfield was shot by a disgruntled office seeker. Lucretia Garfield, called "Crete" by her family, had contracted malaria just months after inauguration and was convalescing at a seaside town in New Jersey when she learned of the attempt on her husband's life. She rushed to Washington to nurse him, but James, a casualty of antiquated medical practices, passed away two months later of an infected wound. Lucretia became the first first lady to appear at her husband's funeral. (Mary Lincoln did not attend the one for her husband.)

James wrote of his wife, "[She] grows up to every new emergency with fine tact and faultless taste." Her few months in the White House supports his observation. Well educated, she met James when they were classmates in 1849, but they did not marry until 1858. They were briefly separated while James served in the military during the Civil War, but they maintained homes in Washington and Ohio while he was an Ohio representative to the U.S. Congress. Their many children brought them closer, as did their shared interest in literature.

Back in Ohio after James's death, Lucretia prepared his political papers for history by creating a memorial library in their home. It served as a precursor to today's presidential libraries. In her later years, she wrote essays on a variety of topics and became particularly interested in architecture and engineering. She moved to Pasadena, California, in 1901, where she supervised construction of a home in the arts and crafts style designed by the celebrated firm of Greene and Greene.

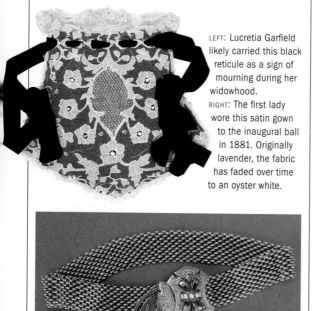

LEFT: Lucretia Garfield likely carried this black reticule as a sign of mourning during her widowhood.
RIGHT: The first lady wore this satin gown to the inaugural ball in 1881. Originally lavender, the fabric has faded over time to an oyster white.

ABOVE: Before her husband became president, Mrs. Garfield wore this gold bracelet inscribed "LRG Jany 1st 1871."

Lucy Hayes was the first first lady to hold a college degree. By the time the Hayes family entered the White House in 1877—after a controversial and contested presidential election—Lucy was a confident wife, mother, political companion, and hostess. Schooled and worldly, she was hailed as a "new woman." Lucy did not openly advocate reforms—and she did not support woman's suffrage—but she did not protest when she was adopted as a symbol of the temperance movement or the struggle for higher education for women.

Raised in Ohio, Lucy graduated from the Wesleyan Female College in Cincinnati. She married Rutherford Hayes in 1852. They had a happy marriage and eight children, five of whom lived to be adults. During the Civil War, Rutherford commanded the 23rd Ohio Volunteer Infantry. The soldiers under his command called his wife "Mother Lucy," due to her compassion and care. When Rutherford returned from the war, Lucy supported his political career. She took an interest in his work, accompanying him on official visits to reform schools, asylums, and prisons while he served as governor of Ohio, and she moved to Washington when he was elected to Congress. The White House during the Hayes administration was a joyful place, despite the president's no-liquor policy. Lucy was a cheerful hostess and together with her husband initiated the now-famous White House Easter egg roll, which continues to draw thousands of children to the lawn of the Executive Mansion every spring.

Lucy and Rutherford retired to Ohio in 1881. One of the most popular first ladies, Lucy died in 1889 and was deeply mourned across the nation.

The President & Mrs. Hayes

request the pleasure of

_____

_____ *company*

at dinner on _____

_____ *18____ at ____ o'clock.*

LEFT: Blank dinner invitations like this one were used during the Hayes administration.
BOTTOM LEFT: Oyster plate from the Hayes White House china service. Lucy Hayes worked with artist Theodore Davis to create designs celebrating the plants and animals of America.
RIGHT: Mrs. Hayes appeared in a gold damask and cream satin gown at the White House New Year's reception in 1880.

Some first ladies truly embrace the job, and Julia Grant was one of them. She called her time in the White House "quite the happiest period of my life." Ulysses Grant was elected to the presidency as a war hero and served during a time of peace. As the wife of a general, Julia finally felt settled and secure after years of accompanying her husband to military posts and enduring long separations. She also felt accepted by Washington society, and unlike Mary Lincoln, she appears not to have been ostracized or scorned for her extravagant clothing or lavish receptions. People found her unpretentious and engaging.

Adventurous and athletic, Julia grew up on a slave-holding plantation near St. Louis, Missouri. There she met Grant (she called him "Ulys"), a West Point classmate of her brother Frederick. They became engaged just before the Mexican War in 1844, and his absence delayed the wedding for several years. After resigning his commission in 1854, Ulysses tried various occupations unsuccessfully until the Civil War called him back to military service.

Julia delighted in his victories as a Union general and his status as a beloved hero to northerners and blacks. She was, indeed, his lifelong defender, even when the business investments he made after leaving the White House failed and nearly ruined the family. Ulysses hoped to make up for the financial losses by publishing his memoirs to earn money for Julia and their children. He finished the volume just before his death from cancer in 1885. Julia lived on income from the book, as well as a widow's pension, until her own death in 1902.

LEFT AND OPPOSITE: Julia Grant's evening gown from the early 1870s is made of white silk damask. According to the Grant family, the rose-patterned fabric was a gift from the emperor of China.

CENTER: After his two terms as president ended, Ulysses Grant and his wife Julia embarked on a two-year trip around the world. They were well received throughout Europe and Asia. While in India, Mrs. Grant was presented with this silver perfume house modeled after a temple.

RIGHT: This group portrait painted by William Cogswell shows the Grant children—Jesse, Nellie, Ulysses Jr., and Frederick—posing with their parents in 1867.

MARY TODD LINCOLN

To this day many people have strong opinions about the controversial and tragic first lady Mary Todd Lincoln. Her time in the White House—a period of turmoil for the country and a source of tremendous anxiety for her husband—was marked by personal sadness, including the death of their young son Willie. As a Southerner married to the leader of the Union during the Civil War, Mary was vilified as a traitor by Confederates and mistrusted as a spy by Northerners. Adept and gracious as a hostess, Mary used White House entertainments to bolster the legitimacy and power of the Lincoln administration, but critics questioned the propriety of spending money on parties and decoration in wartime. Her acts of compassion, from visiting wounded soldiers to assisting African American refugees, went largely unnoticed.

Mary Todd was born into a wealthy family in Lexington, Kentucky. Well educated and vivacious, she moved to Springfield, Illinois, at the age of twenty-one to live with her sister. There she met Abraham Lincoln. They were complete opposites in many ways—she was five feet two inches tall and he was six feet four—but the mismatched pair loved politics and each other. Mary had great faith in her husband as he entered the political arena and eventually was elected president. His assassination in April 1865 was her undoing. Mary never ceased mourning his death. Her depression deepened when her son Tad died in 1871. After a brief involuntary stay in a sanatorium, Mary traveled abroad until ill health forced her to return. She died in her sister's Springfield home in 1882.

ABOVE: Mary Lincoln gave this inkwell, which her husband had used, to her dressmaker and confidante Elizabeth Keckly as a keepsake.

LEFT: A carte de visite of Mrs. Lincoln, taken by Mathew Brady in January 1862, shows the dress before it was altered.

TOP: Silver coffee and tea service engraved with Mrs. Lincoln's monogram and the Todd family crest.

ABOVE: Silver carving set with mother-of-pearl handles engraved *MTL*.

OPPOSITE: Mary Lincoln originally wore this two-piece striped taffeta gown in 1862. The dress was later altered with a new day bodice for another wearer. The original bodice no longer exists.

TOP LEFT: Mary Lincoln wore this onyx and gold mourning watch for the rest of her life. TOP RIGHT: Coffee cup from the Lincoln White House china service. BOTTOM LEFT: Paisley cashmere shawl. BOTTOM CENTER: Gold evening purse. BOTTOM RIGHT: Gold lorgnette engraved with Mary Lincoln's monogram.

OPPOSITE: African American dressmaker Elizabeth Keckly is believed to have made Mrs. Lincoln's purple velvet ensemble, which the first lady wore during the winter social season of 1861–1862. All three pieces are piped with white satin. The daytime bodice is trimmed with mother-of pearl buttons, and the evening bodice is edged with lace and chenille fringed braid.

HARRIET REBECCA LANE

Even though she was not a presidential spouse—her uncle, James Buchanan, never married—Harriet Lane understood how to handle Washington society. With poise and sensitivity, the twenty-six year old hosted White House functions during the most divisive time in American history: the period just before the Civil War. Harriet had the tact and intelligence to entertain the Prince of Wales and other important guests, and she maintained an active social schedule at the White House. By the end of Buchanan's term, however, seven states had seceded from the Union. The president and Harriet were relieved to return to their quiet home near Lancaster, Pennsylvania, in 1861.

Orphaned as a young child, Harriet lived with her favorite uncle and guardian, who provided her with a first-class private school education as well as two years at the Visitation Convent in the Georgetown area of Washington, D.C. Harriet enjoyed getting to know Washington society while Buchanan served as secretary of state. When he was minister to the Court of St. James in London in 1854, the lovely, fair-haired Harriet won many admirers, including Queen Victoria.

Vivacious Harriet had many suitors, but she did not marry until she was thirty-five, when she wed banker Henry Johnston. She eventually suffered the death of her uncle, husband, and two sons, but Harriet lived on to become a generous benefactress to the nation, bequeathing her collection of fine art to the Smithsonian Institution and endowing a home for sick children at Johns Hopkins University in Baltimore, Maryland. The Harriet Lane Clinic is now a pioneering facility for pediatric medicine.

ABOVE LEFT: The first lady and her uncle, President Buchanan, used their personal china service, such as this pink and white Sèvres compote, for formal entertaining. ABOVE RIGHT: Harriet Lane selected this white moire taffeta gown trimmed with white satin and lace for her wedding to Henry Johnston in 1866.

OPPOSITE: In 1898, when she was sixty-eight years old, Harriet Lane Johnston wore this midnight-blue velvet gown to a private audience with Queen Victoria. It was designed by Frederick Charles Worth, Paris.

Jane Pierce had already lost her first two sons: Franklin Jr. died in infancy and Frank Robert died from typhoid fever when he was four years old. When her beloved surviving son Benny died in a tragic train accident just weeks before Franklin Pierce's inauguration as president, Mrs. Pierce was stricken with a grief that cast a shadow on her years as first lady. There was no inaugural ball, and Mrs. Pierce was absent from the swearing-in ceremony. Prayer provided some comfort and strength, but she blamed her husband's interest in politics for Benny's death, and she could not reconcile herself to life in the White House. Her aunt performed many of the duties of the first lady. It was two years before she attended official functions, and she struggled through those social events.

Reverend Jesse Appleton, Jane's father, was a Congregational minister from Brunswick, Maine, who had been president of Bowdoin College. After his death, her mother moved the family to New Hampshire. There Jane met Franklin Pierce, who was interested in politics. (Jane deplored them.) He served in the U.S. House of Representatives and Senate. In 1842, heavily influenced by Jane, Franklin retired from politics. After his military service in the Mexican War, however, the Democratic Party selected him as its candidate in the 1852 presidential election. Jane took the news badly—she fainted—but Franklin convinced her that his service to the country would ensure a good future for their son. Benny's death—and the deepening division that propelled the nation into the Civil War—burdened the couple long after they left the White House.

ABOVE: A daguerreotype of Jane Pierce and her adored son Benny.

CENTER: Mrs. Pierce spent the first two years of her time as first lady in deep mourning following the death of her son and often expressed her grief in letters to him. She wore this mourning locket in remembrance of him.

LEFT: Jane Pierce's black tulle and taffeta mourning dress is embroidered with small silver dots.

ABIGAIL POWERS FILLMORE

The first first lady to hold a paying job before her marriage, Abigail Powers was a teacher for most of her twenties. She was working as an instructor at New Hope Academy in New York State when she met Millard Fillmore, a poor indentured servant looking to further his education. Abigail tutored him in basic subjects and encouraged him when he went on to study law. They waited to marry until Millard established himself and was financially stable. After her husband was elected a New York congressman, Abigail finally had time to pursue reading and gardening, and she devoted her days to raising their two children.

When Millard became vice president in 1849, Abigail did not accompany him to Washington because ill health kept her in Buffalo. A little more than a year later, the death of President Zachary Taylor shocked the nation. Millard assumed the reins of leadership, laboring to keep the quickly splintering Union intact. Abigail's continued poor health excused her from fully assuming the role of political hostess in the nation's capital. She delegated many duties of entertaining to her daughter Abby. Abigail did manage to host small groups of influential people, and she made a lasting contribution to future first families by establishing the White House library.

Millard did not have the political support to run for re-election. The Fillmores graciously attended the inauguration of his successor, President Franklin Pierce, on March 4, 1853. The cold weather that snowy day took its toll on Abigail, who came down with pneumonia soon thereafter. She died in late March and was buried in Buffalo, New York.

LEFT: Abigail Fillmore wore this lavender taffeta and white brocade gown. Although her daughter Abby often served as hostess of the presidential mansion, Mrs. Fillmore attended several White House functions each week.

RIGHT: Always interested in the appearance of the first lady, the public could purchase carte-de-visite copies of this photograph of Abigail Fillmore.

SARAH CHILDRESS POLK

When her husband James ran for president, Sarah Polk announced that if he were indeed elected, she would "neither keep house nor make butter." She defied public expectations of a woman's life being dominated by raising children and doing housework. Childless, Sarah created a role for herself as political wife and advisor. She was fortunate to have been sent away to school, a rare experience for girls in the nineteenth century. Armed with an education, she wed James Polk in 1824, and their marriage became both a life partnership and a political union. She had great ambition for them both. "Sarah wouldn't have married me," James once said, "if I'd been satisfied with a clerkship."

When the Polks moved into the White House in 1845, the light-hearted atmosphere that former first lady Julia Tyler had cultivated was dampened. Sarah, a devout Presbyterian, did not dance or drink alcohol, not even at her husband's inaugural ball, but she did acquire many friends and allies, especially if it was in her husband's best interest. She helped James with his speeches and correspondence, and she weighed in on matters of state. White House dinner guests recalled her vocal support of the Mexican War and expansion in the West that would extend U.S. boundaries to the Pacific Ocean.

After James died in 1849, just months after leaving office, Sarah remained at their home in Nashville, Tennessee, where she upheld the memory of her husband for another forty-two years. Possessing intelligence and dignity until her death at age eighty-eight, she was revered as an influential first lady.

ABOVE: Sarah Polk's lace fan.
LEFT: Mrs. Polk wore this light blue brocaded silk dress woven with a design of poinsettias in the late 1840s. It was remade as an evening gown in the 1880s.
CENTER: Sarah Polk's French porcelain dessert service, made by Dagoty-Honoré, was the first to use the shield of the United States with the national motto *E pluribus unum* (out of many, one).

Julia Gardiner must have been irresistibly charming because President Tyler, a recent widower who was thirty years her senior, quickly proclaimed his love for the twenty-two-year old society girl from a prominent New York family. Their marriage in 1844 was the first of a sitting president. The new Mrs. Tyler embraced the role of first lady, holding receptions and parties until John's term ran out eight months later. As a teenager, the flirtatious girl called herself the "Rose of Long Island" and shocked her family by modeling for a clothing advertisement. Humiliated by her scandalous behavior, her parents whisked her away to Europe. As first lady, she curried favor with the press, leading to descriptions of her in print as "the lovely lady Presidentress"and "her serene loveliness."

After leaving Washington, the Tylers returned to his plantation home, Sherwood Forest, in Virginia. The couple eventually had seven children. (He already had eight children with his first wife, Letitia.) John's death in 1862 was a tremendous loss to his widow, who promoted her husband for years afterward and even signed some of her correspondence with the proud title "Mrs. Ex-President Tyler." An adopted Southerner, Julia defended the institution of slavery and worked for the Confederacy even after the Civil War caused her to evacuate to her family's home in New York. Although Sherwood Forest survived the war, the Tyler family suffered financial setbacks. Ever resourceful, Julia used her influence in Washington to persuade Congress to grant her a presidential widow's pension of $1,200 per year. She died in Richmond, Virginia, in 1889.

ABOVE: Silver calling card case. First ladies routinely paid calls on the wives of congressmen, cabinet officers, and members of the diplomatic corps.

RIGHT: In 1843, a year before she married John Tyler, Julia Gardiner wore an embroidered mull gown when she was presented at the court of Louis Phillipe of France during a European tour.

John Tyler unexpectedly took office following the sudden death of President William Henry Harrison in 1841, but Letitia Tyler was not able to take part in the social affairs of her husband's administration. A stroke two years earlier had left her partially paralyzed, and her daughter-in-law Priscilla Cooper Tyler, at the age of twenty-four, assumed the official duties with confidence and pleasure. Letitia kept to the second floor of the White House, where she engaged in family activities. Priscilla wrote admiringly of her mother-in-law as "the most entirely unselfish person you can imagine.... Notwithstanding her very delicate health, mother attends to and regulates all the household affairs and all so quietly that you can't tell when she does it."

Letitia was born on a Tidewater Virginia plantation in 1790. With little formal education, she learned domestic skills, such as how to maintain a household, care for a husband, and raise children. (She eventually had eight.) She met John, who was then a law student, in 1808, and they married after a five-year courtship. Letitia ably presided over their Williamsburg home while John served both in Congress and as governor of Virginia.

In 1841 John became Harrison's vice president, and Letitia moved to Washington. He was the first vice president to assume the presidency without being elected, which led many people to call him "His Accidency." There is no record of what Letitia thought about the nickname or the role of first lady. She died at the White House on September 10, 1842, halfway through John's first presidential term, and was buried at her family's Virginia estate.

ABOVE: George Bagby Matthews based this 1885 oil painting of Letitia Tyler on an earlier portrait. Her son Robert Tyler and daughter-in-law Priscilla owned this portrait of the first lady.

ABOVE: John Tyler gave Letitia this coral and gold pin in the shape of a spray of willow oak leaves and acorns. Her daughter Alice, who was fourteen when she lived in the White House, inherited this piece of jewelry.

LOUISA JOHNSON ADAMS

Although she was a citizen, the United States was actually a foreign country to Louisa Johnson, who was born in London in 1775 to an English mother and American father. After marrying dour John Quincy Adams, an American diplomat, Louisa lived with her husband in Berlin before they moved to his family home in Quincy, Massachusetts. There she met her opinionated mother-in-law, the feisty former first lady Abigail Adams. When John Quincy's career later called for them to move to Russia, Louisa left her older children to attend school in Massachusetts and took two-year-old Charles with her to the tsar's court, where they struggled with strange customs and cold winters. John Quincy's diplomatic roles repeatedly uprooted the family. In 1815 Louisa and Charles made an arduous forty-day trek by sleigh across Europe in the dead of winter to join him in Paris.

When he was appointed secretary of state in 1817, John Quincy and Louisa finally settled in Washington. Louisa was a confident hostess to government leaders and diplomats. An accomplished harpist, she often performed during gatherings. By the time her husband was elected to the office that his father, John Adams, had held more than twenty years earlier, Louisa suffered from severe bouts of depression and called the White House her "dull and stately prison."

John Quincy lost his bid for re-election in 1828, but he later served in Congress for seventeen years. During his distinguished career as a U.S. representative, both he and Louisa reclaimed some of the respect and happiness that had been denied them in the White House.

LEFT: Louisa Adams's satin dress. TOP CENTER: John Quincy Adams may have purchased a French porcelain service made for the Duca di Mondragone, hence the dragon motif, while in Russia from 1809 to 1814. Louisa Adams used this tureen for formal entertaining.
CENTER LEFT: Mrs. Adams's gold earring. CENTER RIGHT: "Sally" belonged to Louisa's granddaughter, Maria Louisa Adams, the first child born in the White House.
RIGHT: Mrs. Adams frequently entertained her guests after dinner by playing the harp.

ELIZABETH KORTRIGHT MONROE

Elizabeth Monroe's reserved nature and European style were difficult for Washington's elite to accept after enjoying years of Dolley Madison's lavish open houses, but poor health caused her to scale back on entertaining and paying formal calls to politicians and diplomats during the two terms her husband, James Monroe, was in office. Born in 1768 in New York, Elizabeth was the daughter of a man who served the British during the French and Indian War and took no part in the American Revolution. This did not deter James, a revolutionary patriot, from seeking her hand in marriage. She was beautiful and young—only eighteen—when the two wed in 1786.

Elizabeth is best remembered for an incident that occurred before the Monroes arrived in Washington. When her husband served as U.S. minister to France, she accompanied him to Paris, which was in the midst of the bloody French Revolution. There, she went to the prison and dared to visit Madame de Lafayette, the wife of the Marquis de Lafayette, a famous hero of the American War of Independence. The French noblewoman might have been taken to the guillotine, but the timely visit by the wife of an American diplomat spared Madame de Lafayette the fate of so many other aristocrats of that time.

Elizabeth and James Monroe's daughter Maria was the first person married in the White House. The Monroe administration was a peaceful time for the country. After eight years in Washington, the couple returned to Oak Hill, their plantation in Virginia. Elizabeth died there on September 23, 1830.

LEFT: James Monroe gave this topaz necklace to his wife Elizabeth as a gift during their time as a diplomatic couple in France. The French called the beautiful ambassadress "la belle americaine."

CENTER: Elizabeth and James Monroe ordered the first official set of White House china in 1817. The French service, made by the firm of Dagoty-Honoré, pairs the arms of the United States with border vignettes that represent commerce, agriculture, art, science, and warfare. In the Monroe White House, formal receiving lines replaced the casual receptions held by Dolley and James Madison.

RIGHT: Mrs. Monroe's taffeta brocade dress.

DOLLEY PAYNE TODD MADISON

Raised in a strict and sober Quaker household, Dolley Madison exuded warmth and gaiety as first lady. Born in 1768 in North Carolina, Dolley grew up in Virginia and moved to Philadelphia at age fifteen. She was a young widow with one son when she met "the great little Madison." They married in 1794. James represented Virginia in the U.S. Congress, and Dolley became a popular fixture in the nation's capital.

She skillfully navigated Washington society and established the political importance of the White House hostess. Her Wednesday evening "crushes," or drawing room gatherings, brought together politicians, diplomats, and local residents. They became so fashionable and crowded that some people called them "squeezes." Even the most hardened opponents of the Madison administration attended these elaborate affairs over which Dolley presided, often wearing her distinctive turbans and brightly colored gowns.

When the War of 1812 brought British soldiers marching into Washington in 1814, Dolley hastily oversaw the evacuation of the White House. Departing just before enemy troops seized and torched the presidential mansion, she saved from destruction important government documents as well as a full-length portrait of George Washington by artist Gilbert Stuart.

After her husband's death in 1836, Dolley remained an esteemed figure in the nation's capital. At her funeral in 1849, President Zachary Taylor proclaimed, "She will never be forgotten because she was truly our First Lady for a half-century." It was, perhaps, the first official reference to a president's spouse as "first lady."

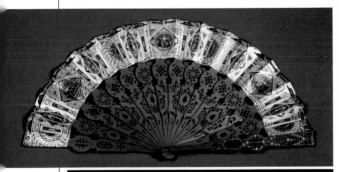

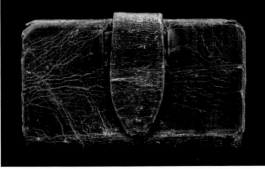

ABOVE: After the White House was burned in 1814, the Madisons revived the capital's social life from a borrowed house. They used a French porcelain dinner and dessert service, including this dish, for official entertaining.
RIGHT: Mrs. Madison's silk satin robe is hand-embroidered with flowers, butterflies, dragonflies, and phoenixes.

TOP: The first lady's painted sandalwood and paper fan was part of her extensive wardrobe that included colorful turbans and gowns from Paris.
ABOVE: In a personal form of politics, Dolley Madison spent her afternoons visiting friends, relations, and the wives of Washington officials. This case held her calling cards.

Despite her lack of formal education, Abigail Smith was curious, intelligent, and well read. This made her a very compatible mate for Harvard-educated lawyer John Adams. Although their marriage was marked by long separations—he was a circuit court judge, a delegate to the Continental Congress in Philadelphia, and then a diplomat in Paris and the Netherlands—the two exchanged lively letters. She described her work to manage their farm in Braintree, Massachusetts, raise their children, and keep them safe during those revolutionary times; he detailed the excitements and frustrations of creating a new government.

A minister's daughter born in 1744 in New England, Abigail Adams was the first first lady to live in the President's Mansion in Washington, now known as the White House. When the Adams family arrived there in 1800, the unfinished building was barely habitable. John's term as president was not without strife. He was considered vain and stubborn, and he made several political enemies. Abigail's interest in political affairs and her outspoken defense of her husband caused some to criticize her for exerting too much influence. Still, most people admired the wit and grit of the woman who reminded her famous mate to "remember the ladies" when he was forming a new code of laws for post-revolutionary society. Abigail had the distinction of being the wife of the second president and the mother of the sixth man to hold that position, John Quincy Adams. She and John were married fifty years, despite the fact that before they were wed, he sent her a list of her "Faults, Imperfections, [and] Defects."

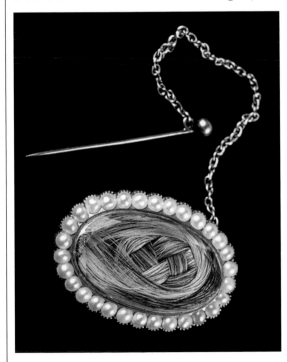

ABOVE: A brooch owned by Abigail Adams contains a lock of her hair as well as locks from her husband John and her son John Quincy. This was a common memento of a loved one.
OPPOSITE: Abigail Adams might have worn this Canton crepe day dress.

TOP: Sauce dish from a Sèvres china service that Abigail and John Adams purchased while he was minister to France in 1784. Abigail joined her husband in his diplomatic posts in France and England.
ABOVE: Yellow kid slippers with brown embroidery worn by Abigail Adams.

MARTHA DANDRIDGE CUSTIS WASHINGTON

As the wife of the first president, Martha Washington established a new social style, one dignified and formal without being "royal," that would command respect for the young republic. George Washington entertained American political leaders and European diplomats. He urged his wife to hold "drawing room" receptions every Friday to host these distinguished guests. Setting aside her own desire for privacy, she welcomed them at the presidential homes in New York and Philadelphia. Knowing that her husband's loyalty to the nation and the ideals of the new United States took precedence, she wrote, "I am still determined to be cheerful and happy, in whatever situation I may be." The first first lady was well aware that hers was a public role of political importance.

Born on June 2, 1731, near Williamsburg, Virginia, Martha Dandridge had little education but was trained in the domestic skills of how to run a household and manage a family. Her first husband, Daniel Parke Custis, died in 1757, leaving her a wealthy widow with two young children. Two years later she married one of Virginia's most eligible landowners, George Washington. Martha dutifully followed her husband to military headquarters and army camps during the Revolutionary War. When the general of the Continental Army became president of the United States, she became known as "Lady Washington."

After two terms, the Washingtons retired to Mount Vernon, their country home in Virginia, in 1797. George died there in 1799. Martha burned their letters, thus ensuring their private life would always remain so. She died on May 22, 1802.

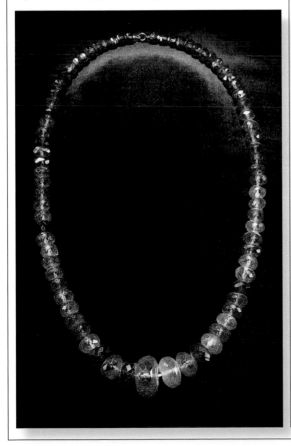

ABOVE: The Washingtons purchased a Sèvres banquet service from the Count de Moustier upon his retirement as French minister in 1790. They used this china service in the presidential mansions in New York City and Philadelphia. The new first family enjoyed a routine of weekly entertainment including a dinner, a gentlemen's reception, and Mrs. Washington's Friday night drawing room gatherings. This set a precedent for future presidential entertaining. LEFT: An amber bead necklace owned by Martha Washington. OPPOSITE: Martha Washington wore this silk taffeta gown in the early 1780s. The silk is hand-painted with a design of flowers and fifty-eight butterflies and insects. The fichu and cuffs are reproductions.

TOP: John Trumbull painted these cabinet portraits of George and Martha Washington around 1793. Likely a gift from the American artist, the couple hung the oil paintings in their bedroom at Mount Vernon.

CENTER LEFT: The Washingtons used this glassware in the presidential mansions and at Mount Vernon.

CENTER RIGHT: Martha Washington's sewing case. She prided herself on her sewing skill and taught her granddaughter Nelly to sew.

BOTTOM LEFT: This saucer from the "States" china was a gift to Mrs. Washington in 1796. Her monogram appears in the center. The names of the fifteen states then in existence decorate the rim.

OPPOSITE: An alternate view of Mrs. Washington's gown.

MARTHA DANDRIDGE CUSTIS WASHINGTON
Born New Kent County, Virginia, June 2, 1731
Died May 22, 1802
First lady 1789–1797, wife of George Washington
Became first lady at age 57
Courtesy of Library of Congress

ABIGAIL SMITH ADAMS
Born Weymouth, Massachusetts, November 11, 1744
Died October 28, 1818
First lady 1797–1801, wife of John Adams
Became first lady at age 52
Courtesy of Library of Congress

MARTHA JEFFERSON RANDOLPH
Born Monticello, Virginia, September 27, 1772
Died October 10, 1836
First lady 1801–1809, daughter of Thomas Jefferson
Became first lady at age 28

DOLLEY PAYNE TODD MADISON
Born Guilford County, North Carolina, May 20, 1768
Died July 12, 1849
First lady 1809–1817, wife of James Madison
Became first lady at age 40
Courtesy of Library of Congress

ELIZABETH KORTRIGHT MONROE
Born New York, New York, June 30, 1768
Died September 23, 1830
First lady 1817–1825, wife of James Monroe
Became first lady at age 48
Courtesy of Library of Congress

LOUISA JOHNSON ADAMS
Born London, England, February 12, 1775
Died May 15, 1852
First lady 1825–1829, wife of John Quincy Adams
Became first lady at age 50
Courtesy of Library of Congress

EMILY DONELSON

Born Donelson, Tennessee, June 1, 1807

Died December 19, 1836

First lady 1829–1831, niece of Andrew Jackson

Became first lady at age 21

Courtesy of White House Historical Association (White House Collection)

SARAH YORKE JACKSON

Born Philadelphia, Pennsylvania, July 16, 1803

Died August 23, 1887

First lady 1831–1837, daughter-in-law of Andrew Jackson

Became first lady at age 31

Courtesy of White House Historical Association (White House Collection)

ANGELICA SINGLETON VAN BUREN

Born Wedgefield, South Carolina, February 13, 1818

Died December 29, 1877

First lady 1839–1841, daughter-in-law of Martin Van Buren

Became first lady at age 21

Courtesy of White House Historical Association (White House Collection)

ANNA SYMMES HARRISON

Born Morristown, New Jersey, July 25, 1775

Died February 25, 1864

First lady 1841, wife of William Henry Harrison

Became first lady at age 65

Courtesy of Library of Congress

LETITIA CHRISTIAN TYLER

Born New Kent County, Virginia, November 12, 1790

Died September 10, 1842

First lady 1841–1842, first wife of John Tyler

Became first lady at age 50

JULIA GARDINER TYLER

Born Gardiner's Island, New York, May 4, 1820

Died July 10, 1889

First lady 1844–1845, second wife of John Tyler

Became first lady at age 24

SARAH CHILDRESS POLK
Born Murfreesboro, Tennessee, September 4, 1803
Died August 14, 1891
First lady 1845–1849, wife of James Polk
Became first lady at age 41
Courtesy of Library of Congress

MARY ELIZABETH TAYLOR BLISS
Born Louisville, Kentucky, April 20, 1824
Died July 25, 1909
First lady 1849–1850, daughter of Zachary Taylor
Became first lady at age 24

ABIGAIL POWERS FILLMORE
Born Stillwater, New York, March 13, 1798
Died March 30, 1853
First lady 1850–1853, wife of Millard Fillmore
Became first lady at age 52
Courtesy of Library of Congress

JANE APPLETON PIERCE
Born Hampton, New Hampshire, March 12, 1806
Died December 2, 1863
First lady 1853–1857, wife of Franklin Pierce
Became first lady at age 46
Courtesy of Library of Congress

HARRIET REBECCA LANE
Born Mercersburg, Pennsylvania, May 9, 1830
Died July 3, 1903
First lady 1857–1861, niece of James Buchanan
Became first lady at age 26
Courtesy of Library of Congress

MARY TODD LINCOLN
Born Lexington, Kentucky, December 13, 1818
Died July 16, 1882
First lady 1861–1865, wife of Abraham Lincoln
Became first lady at age 42
Courtesy of Library of Congress

MARTHA JOHNSON PATTERSON

Born Greeneville, Tennessee, October 25, 1828

Died July 10, 1901

First lady 1865–1869, daughter of Andrew Johnson

Became first lady at age 36

Courtesy of Andrew Johnson National Historic Site, Greeneville, Tennessee

JULIA DENT GRANT

Born St. Louis, Missouri, January 26, 1826

Died December 14, 1902

First Lady 1869–1877, wife of Ulysses Grant

Became first lady at age 43

Courtesy of Library of Congress

LUCY WEBB HAYES

Born Chillicothe, Ohio, August 28, 1831

Died June 25, 1889

First lady 1877–1881, wife of Rutherford Hayes

Became first lady at age 45

Courtesy of Library of Congress

LUCRETIA RUDOLPH GARFIELD

Born Hiram, Ohio, April 19, 1832

Died March 14, 1918

First lady 1881, wife of James Garfield

Became first lady at age 48

Courtesy of Library of Congress

MARY ARTHUR MCELROY

Born Greenwich, New York, July 5, 1841

Died January 8, 1917

First lady 1881–1885, sister of Chester Arthur

Became first lady at age 40

Courtesy of White House Historical Association (White House Collection)

FRANCES FOLSOM CLEVELAND

Born Buffalo, New York, July 21, 1864

Died October 29, 1947

First lady 1886–1889 and 1893–1897, wife of Grover Cleveland

Became first lady at age 21

Courtesy of Library of Congress

CAROLINE SCOTT HARRISON
Born Oxford, Ohio, October 1, 1832
Died October 25, 1892
First lady 1889–1892, wife of Benjamin Harrison
Became first lady at age 56
Courtesy of Library of Congress

IDA SAXTON MCKINLEY
Born Canton, Ohio, June 8, 1847
Died May 26, 1907
First lady 1897–1901, wife of William McKinley
Became first lady at age 49
Courtesy of Library of Congress

EDITH CAROW ROOSEVELT
Born Norwich, Connecticut, August 6, 1861
Died September 30, 1948
First lady 1901–1909, second wife of Theodore Roosevelt
Became first lady at age 39
Courtesy of Library of Congress

HELEN HERRON TAFT
Born Cincinnati, Ohio, June 2, 1861
Died May 22, 1943
First lady 1909–1913, wife of William Taft
Became first lady at age 47
Courtesy of Library of Congress

ELLEN AXSON WILSON
Born Savannah, Georgia, May 15, 1860
Died August 6, 1914
First lady 1913–1914, first wife of Woodrow Wilson
Became first lady at age 52
Courtesy of Library of Congress

EDITH BOLLING GALT WILSON
Born Wytheville, Virginia, October 15, 1872
Died December 28, 1961
First lady 1915–1921, second wife of Woodrow Wilson
Became first lady at age 43
Courtesy of Library of Congress

FLORENCE KLING HARDING
Born Marion, Ohio, August 15, 1860
Died November 21, 1924
First lady 1921–1923, wife of Warren Harding
Became first lady at age 60
Courtesy of Library of Congress

GRACE GOODHUE COOLIDGE
Born Burlington, Vermont, January 3, 1879
Died July 8, 1957
First lady 1923–1929, wife of Calvin Coolidge
Became first lady at age 44
Courtesy of Library of Congress

LOU HENRY HOOVER
Born Waterloo, Iowa, March 29, 1874
Died January 7, 1944
First lady 1929–1933, wife of Herbert Hoover
Became first lady at age 54
Courtesy of Library of Congress

ANNA ELEANOR ROOSEVELT
Born New York, New York, October 11, 1884
Died November 7, 1962
First lady 1933–1945, wife of Franklin Roosevelt
Became first lady at age 48
Courtesy of Library of Congress

ELIZABETH WALLACE TRUMAN
Born Independence, Missouri, February 13, 1885
Died October 18, 1982
First lady 1945–1953, wife of Harry Truman
Became first lady at age 60
Courtesy of Library of Congress

MAMIE DOUD EISENHOWER
Born Boone, Iowa, November 14, 1896
Died November 1, 1979
First lady 1953–1961, wife of Dwight Eisenhower
Became first lady at age 56
Courtesy of Library of Congress

JACQUELINE BOUVIER KENNEDY

Born Southampton, New York, July 28, 1929

Died May 19, 1994

First lady 1961–1963, wife of John Kennedy

Became first lady at age 31

Courtesy of Library of Congress

CLAUDIA TAYLOR JOHNSON

Born Karnack, Texas, December 22, 1912

Died July 11, 2007

First lady 1963–1969, wife of Lyndon Johnson

Became first lady at age 50

Courtesy of LBJ Presidential Library

THELMA RYAN NIXON

Born Ely, Nevada, March 16, 1912.

Died June 22, 1993

First lady 1969–1974, wife of Richard Nixon

Became first lady at age 56

Courtesy of Library of Congress

ELIZABETH BLOOMER FORD

Born Chicago, Illinois, April 8, 1918

Died July 8, 2011

First lady 1974–1977, wife of Gerald Ford

Became first lady at age 56

Courtesy of Library of Congress

ROSALYNN SMITH CARTER

Born Plains, Georgia, August 18, 1927

First lady 1977–1981, wife of Jimmy Carter

Became first lady at age 49

Courtesy of Library of Congress

NANCY DAVIS REAGAN

Born New York, New York, July 6, 1921

First lady 1981–1989, wife of Ronald Reagan

Became first lady at age 59

Courtesy of Library of Congress

BARBARA PIERCE BUSH
Born Bronx, New York, June 8, 1925
First lady 1989–1993, wife of George H. W. Bush
Became first lady at age 63
Courtesy of Library of Congress

HILLARY RODHAM CLINTON
Born Park Ridge, Illinois, October 26, 1947
First lady 1993–2001, wife of William Clinton
Became first lady at age 45
Courtesy of Library of Congress

LAURA WELCH BUSH
Born Midland, Texas, November 4, 1946
First lady 2001–2009, wife of George W. Bush
Became first lady at age 54
Courtesy of the White House

MICHELLE ROBINSON OBAMA
Born Chicago, Illinois, January 17, 1964
First lady 2009–, wife of Barack Obama
Became first lady at age 45
Courtesy of the White House

FRONT COVER
Mamie Eisenhower's 1953 inaugural ball gown, Gift of Mrs. Dwight D. Eisenhower, negative number ET2010-25857

TITLE PAGE
Laura Bush's 2001 inaugural ball gown, Gift of Laura Welch Bush; Rosalynn Carter's 1977 inaugural ball gown, Gift of Mrs. Rosalynn Carter, negative number ET2010-25797

CONTENTS
Caroline Harrison's evening gown, Gift of Mrs. William Henry Harrison, Sr., negative number ET2011-45063

Pg. 12
Clockwise from top left: Emily Donelson's dress, Gift of Mrs. Moncure Burke, negative number 72-2408; Martha Jefferson Randolph's shawl, Gift of Miss Fanny Burke, negative number 72-2403; Sarah Yorke Jackson's dress, Gift of Mrs. James J. McCutcheon, negative number 72-2409; Betty Taylor Bliss's dress, Gift of Miss Mary S. Buchanan, negative number 72-2414; Angelica Singleton Van Buren's dress, Gift of Mrs. Helen Coles Singleton Green, negative number 72-2410; Martha Johnson Patterson's burnous, Gift of Mrs. William T. Bartlett, negative number 72-2419

MICHELLE ROBINSON OBAMA
Pp. 16 and 18
Inaugural ball gown, 2009, Gift of Jason Wu in honor of First Lady Michelle Obama, negative numbers ET2010-25704 and ET2010-25715
Pg. 19
Inaugural ball earrings and "Michelle" signet ring designed by Lorre Rodkin, Gift of Loree Rodkin in honor of First Lady Michelle Obama, negative numbers ET2010-26106 and ET2010-26118
Inaugural ball shoes, Gift of Jimmy Choo in honor of First Lady Michelle Obama, negative number ET2010-25664

LAURA WELCH BUSH
Pg. 20
Inaugural ball gown and purse, 2001, Gift of Laura Welch Bush, negative numbers ET2010-25796 and ET2010-25652
Pg. 21
Bush White House china service plate, Gift of the White House Historical Association, negative number RWS2011-03486
Campaign button, 2000, negative number 2008-5469

HILLARY RODHAM CLINTON
Pg. 22
Inaugural ball gown, 1993, Gift of Hillary Rodham Clinton and the Presidential Inaugural Committee of 1993, negative number ET2010-25723
Pg. 23
Health Security booklet, Gift of Hillary Rodham Clinton, negative number 2004-10212
Hillary for President bumper sticker, negative number

AHB2013q013171
Senate campaign button, 2000, negative number 2008-5470

BARBARA PIERCE BUSH
Pg. 24
Inaugural ball gown, 1989, Gift of Barbara Bush, negative number ET2010-25818
Pg. 25
Campaign button, 1992, negative number 2008-5464
Millie's Book, negative number AHB2009q15003

NANCY DAVIS REAGAN
Pg. 26
Inaugural ball gown and shoes, 1981, Gift of Nancy Reagan, negative numbers ET2010-25743 and ET2010-25657
Suit, Gift of Adolfo Sardina, negative number ET2011-45115
Pg. 27
Press guide to the First Ladies Conference on Drug Abuse, negative number AHB2013q013172
Reagan White House china coffee cup and saucer, Gift of the White House, negative number RWS2011-03497

ROSALYNN SMITH CARTER
Pg. 28
Inaugural ball gown and purse, 1977, Gift of Mrs. Rosalynn Carter, negative numbers ET2010-25806 and ET2010-25651
Pg. 29
Painting of Rosalynn and Amy Carter, Gift of Mary Eve Brockman, negative number 2008-5251
Campaign button, 1977, Gift of Mr. Carl Sferrazza, negative number 2008-5472

ELIZABETH BLOOMER FORD
Pg. 30
State dinner dress, Gift of Elizabeth B. Ford, negative number 2008-5268
Pg. 31
ERA button, negative number AHB2013q013034
Campaign button, 1976, negative number 2008-5465

THELMA RYAN NIXON
Pg. 32
Inaugural ball gown and shoes, 1969, Gift of Mrs. Richard M. Nixon, negative numbers ET2010-25734 and ET2010-25660
Pg. 33
Campaign button, 1960, negative number 2008-5466
Nixon-Cox wedding invitation, Gift of the White House, negative number 2001-12086

CLAUDIA TAYLOR JOHNSON
Pg. 34
Inaugural ball coat and gown, 1965, Gift of Mrs. Lyndon B. Johnson, negative numbers ET2010-25736 and ET2011-45092

Pg. 35
"Our Mineral Heritage" brooch, Gift of the National Gem and Mineral Show Executive Committee, negative number 78-9140
Campaign pamphlet, Gift of the Democratic National Committee, negative number 2003-5876
Pg. 36
"Lady Bird Special" toy train and postcard, Gift of Mrs. Alvin E. O'Konski and Mrs. Chet Holifield, negative numbers 2003-5876 and AHB2010q08577
"Lady Bird Special" breakfast invitation, Gift of Ralph E. Becker, negative number AHB2010q08576
Pg. 37
Johnson-Nugent wedding cake box, Gift of the White House, negative number 2000-7072
Johnson White House china service plate, Gift of the White House, negative number RWS2011-03471
Johnson-Robb wedding invitation, Gift of the White House, negative number 2001-12087

JACQUELINE BOUVIER KENNEDY
Pg. 38
Detail of inaugural ball gown, negative number ET2010-25807; inaugural ball gown and cape, 1961, Gift of Mrs. John F. Kennedy, negative numbers ET2010-25812 and 2006-26853
Pg. 40
Evening dress and state dinner dress, Gift of Oleg Cassini, negative numbers 2004-6240 and 2008-9513
Pg. 41
White House musical program, Gift of Ralph E. Becker, negative number 2003-5896
Pearl necklace, Gift of Lynda and Stewart Resnick and the Franklin Mint, negative number 2008-6471

MAMIE DOUD EISENHOWER
Pg. 42
Inaugural ball gown and shoes, 1953, Gift of Mrs. Dwight D. Eisenhower, negative numbers ET2010-25830 and ET2010-25658
Pg. 43
White House musical program, Gift of Ralph E. Becker, negative number 2003-5891
Campaign button, 1952, negative number 2008-5468
Eisenhower White House china service plate, Gift of Castleton China, Inc., negative number 2004-11135

ELIZABETH WALLACE TRUMAN
Pg. 44
Inaugural reception gown, 1949, Gift of Mrs. Harry S. Truman, negative number 89-2190
Pg. 45
Truman White House china, Gift of Lenox Inc., negative number 2004-5696

ANNA ELEANOR ROOSEVELT
Pg. 46
Inaugural ball gown, 1933, Gift of Mrs. Franklin Delano Roosevelt, negative numbers ET2011-45096 and ET2011-45073
Pg. 47
Sunglasses, Gift of The Andrew H. and Walter R. Beardsley Foundation, negative number 2008-5461
Mink coat, Gift of the Woman's National Democratic Club, negative number 96-2187
Inaugural reception gown, 1945, Gift of Mrs. Franklin Delano Roosevelt, negative number 2004-6241.2

LOU HENRY HOOVER
Pg. 48
Evening gown, Gift of the Hon. Herbert Hoover, negative number ET2011-45078
Pg. 49
Lorgnette, Gift of Mrs. Herbert Hoover, negative number 2004-6242
Floral dress, Gift of Margaret Hoover Brigham, negative numbers ET2011-45110 and ET2011-45112 (detail)

GRACE GOODHUE COOLIDGE
Pg. 50
Evening dress, Gift of Lillian Rogers Parks, negative numbers ET2011-45101 and ET2011-25102
Pg. 51
Purse, Gift of the Estate of Grace Loretto Medinus, negative number 2003-29111
Hand mirror, Gift of Lillian Rogers Parks, negative number 2008-6457
Pg. 52
Evening dress, Gift of Lillian Rogers Parks, negative number 2004-4492
Pg. 53
TL: Pi Beta Phi pin, Gift of Mrs. Calvin Coolidge, negative number 77-3151
TR: Evening dress, Gift of Mrs. Calvin Coolidge, negative number 2000-9314
BL: Dress, Gift of Lillian Rogers Parks, negative number ET2011-45105
BR: Shoes, Gift of Mrs. Calvin Coolidge, negative number 2000-6337

FLORENCE KLING HARDING
Pg. 54
Photograph of Florence Harding with Al Jolson, Gift of the Estate of Dorothy H. Christian, negative number AHB2013q013175
Evening gown, Gift of Mrs. Walter E. Hane, negative number 91-19798

EDITH BOLLING GALT WILSON
Pg. 55
Red Cross hat, Gift of the National Trust for Historic Preservation, negative number 2008-5455
Lalique brooch and evening gown, Gift of Mrs. Woodrow Wilson, negative numbers 77-3160 and ET2011-45069
Shoes and fan, Gift of the National Trust for Historic Preservation, negative numbers 2004-5716 and 76-18019

ELLEN AXSON WILSON

Pg. 56

Painting by Ellen Wilson, Gift of Dr. William D. Hoyt, negative number 92-15743

Evening gown, Gift of Miss Margaret W. Wilson, negative number 65-133

HELEN HERRON TAFT

Pg. 57

Manchu-style coat, Gift of Mr. Charles P. Taft, negative number ET2010-25687

Inaugural ball gown, 1909, Gift of Mrs. William H. Taft, negative numbers 2008-5259 and 2008-5266

Lorgnette, Gift of Lillian Rogers Parks, negative number 79-906

EDITH CAROW ROOSEVELT

Pg. 58

Inaugural ball gown, 1905, Gift of Mrs. Richard Derby, negative number ET2011-09323

Pg. 59

Roosevelt White House china dinner plate, Gift of Josiah Wedgwood and Sons, Inc., negative number RWS2011-03443

Paint set, Gift of Mrs. Violet M. Douglas, negative number 2000-7093

Silk calendar, Gift of Ralph E. Becker, negative number 2003-5878

IDA SAXTON MCKINLEY

Pg. 60

Inaugural ball gown, 1901, Gift of Mrs. Mary B. Barber, negative number 76-18018

Pg. 61

Boots, Gift of Mrs. Mary B. Barber, negative number 2004-5714

Slippers, Gift of the Women's Union, Wellesley Congregational Church, negative number 2008-6450

Sheet music, Gift of Ralph E. Becker, negative number 2003-5889

Dance card, Gift of Mrs. Arthur C. Houghton, negative number 2000-7586

CAROLINE SCOTT HARRISON

Pg. 62

Evening gown, Gift of Mrs. William Henry Harrison, Sr., negative number ET2011-45064

Pg. 63

Dinner favor, Transferred from the Library of Congress, negative number 2000-7590

Harrison White House china plate, Gift of Mrs. Dessie Chase Ellis through Miss Louella P. Chase, negative number 2008-10161

Inaugural ball gown, 1889, Gift of Benjamin Harrison McKee and Mrs. Mary McKee Reisinger, negative number 92-1469

FRANCES FOLSOM CLEVELAND

Pg. 64

Evening gown, Gift of Mr. and Mrs. Richard F. Cleveland, negative number 2004-4489

Pg. 65

Merrick Thread ad, Gift of Ralph E. Becker, negative number 2003-5873

Wedding gown, Gift of the Heirs of Richard F. and Jessie B. Cleveland, negative number 92-3649-9

Pg. 66

Floral skirt and bodices, Gift of Mr. and Mrs. Richard F. Cleveland, negative number ET2011-09311 (floral), negative number ET2011-09309 (peach), negative number ET2011-09306 (green)

Pg. 67

Playing cards, Gift of Paul Beckwith, negative number AHB2013q013176

Advertising card, Gift of Ralph E. Becker, negative number 2003-5872

Doll, Gift of Mrs. Frances C. Corcoran, negative number AHB2013q013178

Doll house, Gift of Mrs. Jessie B. Cleveland, negative number 77-12886

LUCRETIA RUDOLPH GARFIELD

Pg. 68

Lace reticule, Gift of Mrs. Herbert Feis, negative number JN2013-2635

Inaugural ball gown, 1881, Gift of Abram, Harry A., Irwin McD., and James R. Garfield and Mary Garfield Stanley-Brown, negative number 91-10693

Bracelet, Gift of Mrs. Herbert Feis, negative number 2004-6242

LUCY WEBB HAYES

Pg. 69

Hayes White House invitation, Gift of The Rutherford B. Hayes Library, negative number 2004-6884

Hayes White House china oyster plate, Gift of Lucille P. Wallshein, negative number 2004-5935

Reception gown, Gift of Colonel Webb C. Hayes, negative number 91-1466-1

JULIA DENT GRANT

Pp. 70 and 71

Evening gown, Gift of Frederick D. Grant, Jesse R. Grant, Ulysses S. Grant, Jr., and Nellie Grant Sartoris, negative numbers ET2010-25692 and ET2010-25688

Pg. 71

Perfume house, Gift of Frederick D. Grant, Jesse R. Grant, Ulysses S. Grant, Jr., and Nellie Grant Sartoris, negative number 2008-10158

Grant family portrait, Gift of Julia Dent Grant and William H. Vanderbilt, negative number MAH-45727

MARY TODD LINCOLN

Pg. 72

Dress, Gift of Mrs. Harold V. Welch, negative number 92-6344

Pg. 73

Inkwell, Gift of Capt. George van Deurs, USN, negative number 2008-5446

Carte de visite, Gift of the Estate of Catalina Juliana Mason Myers James, negative number 2008-6266
Silver tea and coffee service and carving set, Gift of Lincoln Isham, negative numbers 89-8593 and 2008-5473
Pg. 74
Velvet ensemble, Bequest of Mrs. Julian-James, negative numbers ET2011-45126 and 2008-45126
Pg. 75
Mourning watch and Lincoln White House china cup, Gift of Lincoln Isham, negative numbers 2008-6462 and 2008-10163
Paisley shawl, Gift of Mr. Charles Cohen, negative number 2004-4491
Evening purse and lorgnette, Gift of Lincoln Isham, negative numbers 2008-6460 and 2008-6465

HARRIET REBECCA LANE
Pg. 76
Gown, Gift of The Misses Elizabeth Gray, Juliana Paca and Margaret Beverly Taylor, negative number 2004-4495
Pg. 77
Compote, Gift of Talbot T. Speer, negative number 79-835
Wedding gown, Gift of Miss May S. Kennedy, negative number 65-119

JANE APPLETON PIERCE
Pg. 78
Mourning dress, Gift of Mrs. John M. Corse, negative number 72-2416
Locket, Gift of Mary Shipman Mian, negative number 2004-5932

ABIGAIL POWERS FILLMORE
Pg. 79
Dress, Gift of Mrs. J. D. Larkin, negative number 65-117

SARAH CHILDRESS POLK
Pg. 80
Dress, Gift of Mrs. George W. Fall, negative number 2004-6240
Fan, Gift of The Polk Memorial Association, negative number 78-18020
Polk White House china plates, Gift of Mr. and Mrs. B. Woodruff Weaver, negative numbers RWS2011-03454 and RWS2011-03456

JULIA GARDINER TYLER
Pg. 81
Silver card case, Gift of Virginia Gunter Haas Orvis, negative number 2008-6461
Dress, Gift of Mr. Madison E. Marye, Mrs. M. N. Ellis, and Mrs. Marshall P. Stuart, negative number 72-2412

LETITIA CHRISTIAN TYLER
Pg. 82
Portrait of Letitia Tyler, Gift of Letitia C. Arant, negative number 2008-5255
Coral pin, Gift of Mrs. Alice Denison Nicholson, negative number ET2013-40207

LOUISA JOHNSON ADAMS
Pg. 83
Dress, Gift of Mary Louisa Clement, negative number 65-109
Soup tureen, earring, doll, and harp, Gift of Mary Louisa Adams Clement in memory of Louisa Catherine Adams Clement, negative numbers 75-10215 (tureen), RWS2011-00342 (earring), 2000-7091 (doll), and 2008-10687 (harp)

ELIZABETH KORTRIGHT MONROE
Pg. 84
Topaz necklace, Gift of Eleanor D. Hertle, negative number 2008-6470
Monroe White House china dessert plate, negative number RWS2011-03442
Dress, Gift of Camilla Hoes-Pope, negative number 64-107

DOLLEY PAYNE TODD MADISON
Pg. 85
Fan, Gift of Miss Barbara Donald, negative number 77-1049
Card case, Transfer from the Library of Congress, negative number RWS2011-03505
Serving dish, Gift of Miss Mary M. McGuire, negative number 2008-10162
Dress, negative number 91-19795-44

ABIGAIL SMITH ADAMS
Pg. 86
Dress, Gift of Susan E. Osgood, negative number 65-104
Pg. 87
Brooch, Gift of Mr. Richard Cranch Greenleaf, negative number 77-3158
Sauce dish, Gift of Miss Mary Louisa Adams Clement, negative number 2000-7118
Slippers, Gift of Susan E. Osgood, negative number 2008-6451

MARTHA DANDRIDGE CUSTIS WASHINGTON
Pp. 88 and 90
Dress, Gift of Mrs. John McFarland Bergland and Mrs. Asher Abbott White, negative numbers ET2010-25788 and 92-3645-3
Pg. 89
Amber necklace, negative number 97-7907
Serving dish and plate, Transferred from the U.S. Patent Office, negative numbers RWS2011-03433 and RWS2011-03432
Pg. 91
Portraits of George Washington and Martha Washington, Transferred from the U.S. Patent Office, negative numbers 89-6826 and 89-6827
Glassware and saucer, Transferred from the U.S. Patent Office, negative numbers RWS2011-03428 and 72-9967
Needle case, negative number AHB2013q013179

This book may be purchased for educational, business, or sales promotional use. For information, please write:
Special Markets Department
Smithsonian Books
P. O. Box 37012
MRC 513
Washington, DC 20013

Published by Smithsonian Books
Director: Carolyn Gleason
Editor: Christina Wiginton
Editorial Assistant: Ashley Montague

Text by Lisa Kathleen Graddy and Amy Pastan
National Museum of American History staff: Bethanee Bemis, Larry Bird, Alicia Cutler, Debra Hashim, Marilyn Higgins, Patricia Mansfield, Sara Murphy, Jaclyn Nash, Harry Rubenstein, Hugh Talman, Richard Strauss

Edited by Nancy Eickel
Designed by Bill Anton | Service Station

Library of Congress Cataloging-in-Publication Data
Graddy, Lisa Kathleen.
The Smithsonian First Ladies Collection / Lisa Kathleen Graddy and Amy Pastan.
    pages cm
ISBN 978-1-58834-469-4 (pbk.), ISBN 978-1-58834-488-5 (hc)
1. Presidents' spouses–United States–Biography–Miscellanea.
2. Presidents' spouses–United States–History–Exhibitions.
3. National Museum of American History (U.S.)–Exhibitions.
I. Pastan, Amy. II. National Museum of American History (U.S.)
III. Title.
E176.2.G73 2014
973.09'9–dc23   2014000511

Manufactured in the United States of America
18 17 16 15 14   5 4 3 2 1

For permission to reproduce illustrations appearing in this book, please correspond directly with the owners of the works, as seen on this page. Smithsonian Books does not retain reproduction rights for these images individually, or maintain a file of addresses for sources.

FRONT COVER: Mamie Eisenhower's 1953 inaugural gown.
BACK COVER: (from left) Portrait of Martha Washington; Frances Cleveland's wedding gown; Grace Coolidge's evening dress; ERA button; Reagan White House china service plate, gift of the White House, negative number RWS2011-03493; Michelle Obama presenting her gown to the First Ladies Collection in March 2010.

NOTES

The First Ladies Collection
[1] Cassie Mason Myers Julian-James, foreword in Rose Gouverneur Hoes, *Catalogue of American Historical Costumes, Including those of the Mistresses of the White House as Shown in the United States National Museum* (Washington, DC: Waverly Press, 1915), p. i.
[2] Ibid.
[3] Rose Gouverneur Hoes, *The Dresses of the Mistresses of the White House as Shown in the United States National Museum* (Washington, DC: Historical Publishing Company, 1931), p. 3.
[4] Ibid., p. 35.
[5] Ibid., p. 55.
[6] Hoes, *Catalogue of American Historical Costumes*, p. ii.
[7] Smithsonian Institution, Annual Report of the United States National Museum (Washington, DC: Government Printing Office, 1931), p. 110.
[8] Merrie Morris Hammond, "Klapthor's Lifework: First Ladies Gowns," *Washington Times Magazine* (July 30, 1985), p. 6M.

Who is a First Lady?
[1] Rose Gouverneur Hoes, *The Dresses of the Mistresses of the White House as Shown in the United States National Museum* (Washington, DC: Historical Publishing Company, 1931), p. 27.

PHOTO CREDITS